Psalms for a Pilgrim People

Psalms
for a
Pilgrim People

JIM COTTER

MOREHOUSE PUBLISHING

This book was originally published by Cairns Publications, Sheffield, England, in three separate volumes:

Through Desert Places: A version of Psalms 1-150,
copyright © 1989 by Jim Cotter

By Stony Paths: A version of Psalms 51-100,
copyright © 1991 by Jim Cotter

Towards the City: A version of Psalms 101-150,
copyright © 1993 by Jim Cotter

Published in the United States of America by
Morehouse Publishing
P.O. Box 1321
Harrisburg, PA 17105

Morehouse Publishing is a division of The Morehouse Group.

Printed in the United States of America

Cover design by Kirk Bingaman

Library of Congress Cataloging-in-Publication Data
Cotter, Jim.
[Through desert places]
Psalms for a pilgrim people/Jim Cotter.
    p. cm.
    First work originally published: Through desert places.
    Sheffield, England: Cairns Publications, © 1989. 2nd work
    originally published: By stony paths. Sheffield, England : Cairns
    Publications, © 1991. 3rd work originally published: Towards the
    city. Sheffield, England Cairns Publications, © 1993.
    Includes bibliographical references.
    ISBN 0-8192-1778-6 (pbk.)
    1. Bible. O.T. Psalms—Paraphrases, English. I. Cotter, Jim.
By stony paths. II. Cotter, Jim. Towards the city. III. Title.
IV. Title: By stony paths. V. Title: Towards the city.
[BS1440.C68   1998]
223'.205209—dc21   98-42301
                                                            CIP

CONTENTS

FROM THE FOREWORDS
TO THE ORIGINAL VOLUMES

Through Desert Places: A version of Psalms 1-150 (1989)
The new turns of phrase should open to us new insights into the Psalmists' rich and enduring spirituality...What is attempted in this presentation...is a supremely important and necessary task for which we have good reason to be grateful. It deserves to be used painstakingly and attentively in our own pilgrim's progress.
—*Alan Ecclestone,* Anglican priest, harrier of the powers that be, writer on prayer, d.1992

By Stony Paths: A version of Psalms 51-100 (1991)
[This] version is not so much a translation as a re-working, a re-fashioning. It is as if [the writer] has taken a collection of clothes, unpicked them, and then made a new garment out of each... the poet with vivid images and words that sing, the prophet reminding us that we are destroying the earth, and the priest reminding us of God in our midst.
—*Sheila Cassidy,* doctor, notably with the dying, and author
of *Audacity to Believe*

Towards the City: A version of Psalms 101-150 (1993)
...it is the language, above all, which marks this [book] as a truly inclusive collection of prayers. And that does not simply mean that women and men may use them with equal confidence. It means that God too is named in ways which invite us to draw closer to the mystery which Christianity has consolidated by revealing to us the deepest desire of God, namely to be with us—and not apart from us.
—*Lavinia Byrne,* cyber-nun, broadcaster, writer

INTRODUCTION

An Invitation

There is a well-loved radio program in England and the United States called *Desert Island Discs*. Week by week notable people are interviewed about their lives and asked which pieces of music they would take with them to a desert island if they could choose only eight. Some years ago, I worked with a number of parish study groups and asked each member to choose his or her "desert island psalms." So my invitation to you: Before reading any further, which eight psalms would you take with you?

Again and again, the same psalms were chosen, from among a group of thirty-seven. (The thirty-seven are listed at the end of this introduction.) There was an unusual choice from time to time, but no one person's list ever included more than one psalm from outside that range of thirty-seven. What fascinated me at the time was that nearly three-quarters of the Psalter was not chosen at all—apart from occasional verses remembered from an otherwise unmemorable psalm. Moreover, even within the ones selected, people frequently excluded considerable portions.

Do we leave the rest to clergy, monks, and nuns, many of whom say the whole Psalter during the course of a week or a month or two? If not, then we have some work to do to reclaim quite a number of prayers that, though they are in the Bible, are no longer in a form that most people can use. This book invites you to share in that work.

What this book is not—and what it is

But first let me say what you will *not* find in these pages. I do not know more than a few words of Hebrew. I regret this, but the consequence is that I am not able to make a new translation. Nor will you find a modest paraphrase, which would simply draw out the meaning of some of the more difficult words and phrases.

No, what I have tried to do is to "unfold" the Psalms afresh, sometimes only lightly amending what has stood the test of time as good poetry, sometimes incorporating ideas and imagery from the Christian Testament as well as from the Hebrew Scriptures, sometimes quite deliberately arguing, even contradicting—certainly adding to—the original, interweaving the questions and contributions of our own century with what we have inherited from the past.

How to use this book

The Psalms have been laid out on the page so that they can be used either by a person praying alone or by groups and congregations praying together. One voice—or a few—could say or chant the sections, and the whole company could respond with the refrain at the end of each section. There could then be a period of silence before everybody joins in saying the prayer that follows. I have noticed that groups of people tend to shout when reading the Psalms together, and that is a puzzle. Certainly the mood of some of these verses is exultant, and then a shout is indeed appropriate. "Alleluia" and "Yippee" are not far apart in meaning. But surely it is best to be sensitive to the various moods, and on the whole to speak slowly and quietly.

A word or two about the longest psalm: 119! It can seem repetitive and boring—as the statements lovers make to each other seem to the outsider. But ah, if you are the one in love! So this psalm is a love song to the God of Wisdom. It celebrates the Law, the Torah, the Living Way, the whole counsel of the living God in covenant with the people. The twenty-two sections reflect this theme as if they were varying shafts of light from a crystal. In this book they are set out rather differently from the rest of the psalms. There is an introduction printed in italic, which could be read by a solo voice. This is followed by three lines, "The journey" (a word or phrase suggesting an event on life's journey or a stage of the pilgrimage), "The invitation" (from the Gospels, that of Jesus to the people among whom he lived), and "The implication" (a suggestion as to how we might respond if we take both journey and invitation seriously). And the themes are taken up in the section of the psalm that follows. It is important for those of us who have difficulty with the praise of law to remember that we are not dealing with rules and regulations that must be mechanically obeyed in every single detail. Rather do the laws unfold for us certain characteristics of our lives that will become typical once we have responded to the gracious invitation of the living, loving God. Remember this long psalm is a *love song.* (As perhaps can be said of the whole Psalter.)

One further thought: If we in truth belong irrevocably to one another, are interdependent as human beings in a global village, and bound together in the Body of Christ, then we need a form of prayer that can carry us more deeply into that truth. The Psalms can help. They express our common praise of the One who loves us all, and they express our common concerns for one another in intercession. Even when we cannot identify personally with a particular experience described in a psalm, we can make the saying of it into a prayer for those who can.

But perhaps I am getting ahead of myself. You may need convincing that it might be a good idea to try praying through the versions in this book rather than what you already have in your Bible or prayer book.

And shouldn't we keep to the exact words of the Bible?

Our Presbyterian ancestors of the sixteenth century were the first to put the Psalms into English metrical verse. But they were careful not to introduce any other vocabulary than was there in the original. Later hymn writers and compilers of hymnbooks did not feel so constrained. Take Psalm 23, for instance, one of the inevitable "desert island" choices. Many of us know the psalm in the version from the Scottish Psalter of 1650, "The Lord's my shepherd," sung most often to the tune Crimond. Almost equally well known is H.W. Baker's nineteenth-century version, "The King of Love my shepherd is." For a start, neither the word "King" nor the word "Love" occurs in Psalm 23. Baker is letting his faith in Jesus Christ inform the psalm. Hence later we have the line, "Thy cross before to guide me." Similarly, the "sweet and wondrous love" of God is central to George Herbert's seventeenth-century version, "The God of love my shepherd is."

But what of the version, "The Lord my pasture shall prepare"? It is by Joseph Addison, English essayist of the eighteenth century. I wonder if he wrote it while staying for the weekend in a friend's country house, amongst newly laid out gardens and park? After mentioning fainting in "the sultry glebe" (land attached to the parsonage and church)—hardly a landscape the Psalmist would have been familiar with:

> To fertile vales and dewy meads
> My weary wandering steps he leads,
> Where peaceful rivers, soft and slow,
> Amid the verdant landscape flow.

In the next verse we find ourselves among "sudden greens and herbage" and "murmuring" streams, followed at the end by the "aid" of "thy friendly crook," a noun easily misunderstood.

Well, such a version is not untrue to the spirit of the original psalm, but it certainly reflects a time and place now known only in nostalgia by those who, whether English or American, long for a vanished countryside that in fact can have been delectable only to the privileged few. Eighteenth-century rural life was rather different for most of the people who lived and worked there. Lords of the manor were not averse to moving a whole village if it interfered with the view from the mansion.

More seriously, if the Holy Spirit has been promised to guide us into the truth, and the truth is not simply propositions to which we do or do not give our assent, but rather is it discovered in and among human beings living in relationship with one another, then we can expect new unfoldings in each generation, some of which will doubtless be further criticized and changed by the next. We may be in communion with our ancestors of faith, but surely not slavishly. Indeed I would maintain it is our responsibility to listen for and articulate fresh thoughts for a new day, reflections charged with the poetry and passion of our experience, bringing out treasure old and new from the scriptural songs of the past and writing our own as well.

Encouragement from the Psalms themselves

This kind of critical solidarity with our ancestors can be illustrated from within the psalms themselves. Psalm 51 gives a clear example. It is a deeply personal penitential psalm: the sacrifice that God desires is a humbled spirit and a contrite heart. But the two verses at the end are so different in tone that they are now thought to have been added by a later hand. An official in the Temple in Jerusalem? Well, somebody who, while conceding that the right *intention* is necessary in the worshiper, is eager to affirm that animal sacrifices are still important. A touch of ecclesiastical vested interest, I wonder? We might want to ask a similar question, but with our own dilemmas in mind. Can the nonconformist (*my* way of praying) and the conformist (we've always done it this way) both give way to an approach to prayer that recognizes a variety of acceptable ways of praying within a common loyalty to one another and to God, ways that honor the past but seek to transform it?

Further, in our own day we are living with the bewilderment of no longer being able to claim we belong to one overarching culture, and it is an acute question how we can foster the well-being of the one globe with its increasing diversity and complexity. What was once regarded as universal is not now experienced as such, and we rightly fear disintegration. But how do we find our way?

A contribution

Faced with that question, it feels faintly ludicrous for me to be offering this new unfolding. The book has been written by an ordained, English, middle-class, educated man, with the cadences of his native language echoing almost physically in his mind from the sixteenth and seventeenth centuries. Through it, however, the language of the silenced finds some expression because of his roots in some of the first peoples of these islands of northwestern Europe, and because of his experience of the struggles of a sexual minority to find a way of speech that gives some shape and coherence to their experience. But the contribution in these pages can only be partial and temporary. I hope that those who use them find themselves making their own alterations, subtractions, and additions.

These versions of the Psalms are offered as a form of prayer *for the time being*. They have been used in their original editions by a variety of people—from an elderly man quietly musing on his own to a nurse who found some of them an adequate container for her distress at the end of a harrowing day in a hospital—and by congregations who found the Sunday handout containing something unexpected. But doubtless these versions will fade sooner or later: few contemporary prayers last beyond the generation in which they were written. It is good for all of us that that is so.

Praying faithfully today

We human beings are being pressed protestingly into the reality of a citizenship of one world. Each religious tradition is being challenged to look carefully at its tendencies toward being exclusive and hostile to others. If we relish this crisis as opportunity, we may find ourselves willing to use the language and imagery of a global culture in our praying— from the huge issues of nuclear power and ecology on a vulnerable planet to the particular experiences of cars and bicycles, T-shirts and jeans, traffic lights and television, propaganda and sporadic violence, viruses and bacteria in food and bloodstreams— in each and every city of the world.

So, in these versions of the Psalms:

> ...invisible rain falls on the mountains,
> even the caves fill with rubble. (Psalm 11)

> Save us from the corruption of language,

from manipulators of words, greedy for power. (Psalm 12)

In country lanes we have hidden and pounced,
in city streets we have stalked and murdered. (Psalm 10)

The young prowl the streets and the malls,
alienated rootless, pain turning to violence. (Psalm 7)

In the Hebrew Psalm 22, which Jesus may have prayed as he was
dying, there is the picture of the huntsmen and their dogs encircling
their victim. In the version in this book, similar experiences are
added from our own century: the prisoner in the concentration
camp, the patient in the hospital gasping for air, the person
quarantined and left alone by those who withdraw in terror.

Again, with our new understanding of the vastness of the universe:

The beginning was all flame,
and the flame unfurled into time;
all that has come into being
began at the heart of the flame. (Psalm 104)

The laws of God:
...dance as the stars of the universe,
perfect as the parabolas of comets,
like satellites and planets in their orbits,
reliable and constant in their courses. (Psalm 19)

And we human beings are called to be guardians of the planet
that is our home:

How awesome a task you entrust to our hands,
how fragile and beautiful is the good earth. (Psalm 8)

Praying for our "enemies"

When that good earth was more forested than it is now, only
sporadically settled, it is not surprising that those over the mountains
or across the river, unknown and possibly more powerful, were
feared as enemies. Nor is it surprising that wars broke out over
disputed territory as the population grew and the land was cleared.
Only in our generation have we reached the point where

cooperation for the sake of the survival of the planet is rendering war a wasteful, outmoded, and increasingly suicidal means of resolving conflict.

As our consciousness changes, the use of many of the Psalms becomes more and more problematic. They often assume an "over-againstness," of enemies beyond the gate—and of course God is always on our side. "We" are innocent in our integrity while "they" are spurned as hypocrites and deceivers. I suspect that this should sound more shrill and defensive to our ears than it often does, especially when politicians manipulate our patriotism into jingoism. We have suffered—and still do suffer—from so-called "holy" wars.

By contrast, and very slowly over the centuries, we have had glimpses of a different kind of God, one who indeed strives with those who rebel against the ways and laws of Love, but little by little impinges on human beings exactly as a loving rather than a coercive power, one who seeks always to redeem tragedy and to travel the second mile in pursuit of the bewildered, the lost, and the maimed. Our problem is our continuing projection onto God of our suspicion of the stranger, so that we can self-righteously slaughter our enemies on God's behalf.

You can see these two viewpoints struggling with each other in different people's attitudes to the words of Jesus, as reported in chapter 8 of the Gospel according to John, to the woman who had been caught in the act of adultery. Having challenged her accusers to throw the first stone only if they were themselves without sin, he says to the woman, "Neither do I condemn you; go, and do not sin again" (verse 11). I have noticed over the years that some people emphasize the first part of that sentence, others the second. But I wonder what Jesus would have said to the person who asked him, "What if she commits adultery again?" If you focus on, "Go, and do not sin again," you might well say, "She has had a second chance, but now the law must take effect and she must be stoned." If you focus on, "Neither do I condemn you," you might say, "I cannot condemn you even now, even though you are brought to me seventy times seven." But the sorrow in the voice and the hurt in the eyes might make the questioner pause. Here is a man who bears the pain of her wrongdoing and of mine, one who feels it right through to his very being. And in turn that thought might enable the response, "Let me share the pain too. Let me stop acting in ways that hurt you. You are so utterly loving, so totally attractive, that I cannot but love you in return." In such fragmentary moments of reconciliation I think we do from time to time *know* that this is the Gospel Way.

The process of the prayer of recognition and reconciliation

So, if we seek to transform our praying for our enemies in this light, then we must find our way, with clarity and courage, *through* this process of recognition and reconciliation. At least seven stages can be discerned, and they have been incorporated into this new unfolding of the Psalms:

1 Honestly admitting our hostile feelings:

> Slay them with your iron fist,
> may they choke on the grapes of your wrath. (Psalm 17)

Denial of anger never does any good, and it is mealymouthed to pretend that our feelings are any more civilized than those of our ancestors. But of course such anger rarely helps if it is not transformed into a passion for justice and reconciliation. We are challenged *not* to keep ourselves totally separate from those with whom we are so angry.

2 Becoming aware of our own hatreds and potential for evil:

> Purge me of hatred and smugness,
> of self-righteous satisfied smile. (Psalm 17)

This is a discipline of deliberately willing to be less judgmental of others and more sternly truthful with ourselves:

> Forgive the boast of your people, O God,
> self-righteous and blind in our mouthings. (Psalm 26)

3 Becoming aware also of the forces that threaten us from within as well as from others:

> I am afraid of the powers that prowl within me,
> howling in the dark of the moonless nights. (Psalm 3)

4 Recognizing the Love that is expressed through both judgment and mercy:

> You thunder so fiercely in love for us,
> you whisper so gently in judgment. (Psalm 50)

5 Focusing this awareness in contemplation of Christ, recognizing that the extremes of some of our prayer need to be tempered:

> Do not be mocked or derided, O God:
> speak to us in your wrath,
> terrify us in your fury...
>
> But who *is* this, God's Chosen One, God's *Son?*
> Inheritor of the earth and all its people?
> You take our rage upon yourself,
> mocked and crucified, yet meeting all with love. (Psalm 2)

6 Being brought to true repentance, through a clear recognition of ourselves in relation to God:

> Ah, Fire that shrivels up our hates,
> and brings us to our knees in awe!
> Ah, Light that pierces all our fury,
> laying bare our greed and pride!
>
> Forgive us, for we know not what we do. (Psalm 2)

God's Love may be stern but it is not vindictive. In the imagery of fire, it refines but does not utterly destroy. God brings good out of seeming total evil, a good that is beyond our imagining, yet the hope of which can become more securely embedded in our prayer than many of the words we have inherited would lead us to suppose.

7 Offering ourselves, willing a new direction:

> Dear God, we offer you our lives this day,
> the gift of love in our hearts and our loins,
> the incense of prayer, the myrrh of our suffering,
> the gold of all that we hold most dear... (Psalm 45)

Such kindness towards others must needs be extended to our own enemy within:

> Blessed are those who care for the poor and the helpless,
> who are kind to the outcast within them. (Psalm 41)

In some such way I believe it is possible for us to draw closer to the true and living God, overcoming the unnecessary distancing that we can often experience when we try to pray many of the Psalms in their original form.

Claiming the story of our ancestors as our own

There is a further such distancing in those Psalms that retell the details of the stories of the ways in which God is believed to have acted in the lives of the people. Inevitably they do not bring God alive for us in quite such a vivid and immediate way as they did for those who had direct memories of the events. Only if we can imaginatively leap the centuries can we make them part of our own story. Moreover, the history is written in the third person, which makes the psalm more of a description than a prayer.

Two changes can help. One is to alter the grammar so that the words become a more direct prayer to God in I/We—You language. Immediately the psalm engages and involves us more.

The second is to refer to the present and the future as well as to the past, with petition and hope becoming part of the prayer as well as thanksgiving and penitence. We need to take seriously the Hebrew sense of the _continuing_ activity of God: creation is not so much a past event as a ceaseless active process. For example, in this book, Psalm 33 gives a perspective on both history and creation, Psalm 104 reminds us of the continuing processes of creation, and Psalm 105 brings the notion of the covenants of God with the people into the present day.

A call to adventurous faith

These variants and changes are not without risk, for they may betray truth. We must keep on prying open our own twentieth-century assumptions in order that they be tested by past wisdom—just as we must have the courage in our turn to say that our ancestors were sometimes wrong. The Church, like the individuals in it, has never been very good at admitting error. So the task of re-shaping, unfolding, renewing needs to be attempted in a spirit of humility, but it may be more than mere fancy to hope that our ancestors may one day be eager to learn what new things God has revealed to us through our questing spirit in our own generation. It may even be that truth will dawn on us in the midst of the very process of arguing with those half-forgotten and shadowy people of faith.

Years ago my mind stored the sixth verse of Psalm 84 in the Book of Common Prayer of 1662:

> Who going through the vale of misery use it for a well,
> And the pools are filled with water.

Those words haunt me with the hope of their content and the beauty of their expression. But their truth is tough as well as glistening. They challenge us to dig deep into faith's uncompromising terrain, and although there is hope of refreshment, it is in the midst of the desert. Sustained we may be, but to bore a hole for the well is not easy. The drill biting into the rock frequently breaks, and the heat of the day echoes the harsh landscape. It was in such unpromising circumstances, like many of our own, that the Psalms were created, in an anguished trust in a seemingly absent God. It is because of this that they have resonated soul-deep in human beings ever since.

If there is a God, only a pain-bearing God can help. That is the hope—embodied, so we may believe, in God-in-Christ. And that hope keeps alive the possibility of praise.

Many are the afflictions of those who seek good,
but the pain-bearing God is with them.
You penetrate to the heart of their suffering,
that they come to no lasting harm. (Psalm 34)

And in the words of the prayer that follows that psalm:

Pain-bearer God, in our affliction we sense your presence,
moving with our sufferings to redeem them,
bringing joy out of tragedy,
creating such music as the world has not yet heard.
We praise you with great praise.

If such faith holds, it does so only just. And it does so in our very act of falling into an abyss. We do not know whether we shall crash on the rocks, or how fearful it may be to fall into the hands of the living God. We are promised that underneath us are the everlasting arms, but we are not meant to be infants for long. Will the great white bird of the southern ocean that is the Spirit of God seize us and teach us how to fly?

Note: *"Desert Island Psalms"*
Almost invariably the selection came from these thirty-seven: 4, 8, 15, 16, 19, 22, 23, 24, 27, 31, 42, 43, 46, 51, 67, 84, 90, 91, 95, 98, 100, 102, 104, 107, 121, 122, 126, 127, 128, 130, 131, 133, 134, 137, 139, 148, 150.

PSALMS 1-50

THE TWO WAYS – A WISDOM SONG

Refrain: *Keep us true to your Way.*

WOE to us when we walk in the way of wickedness,
when we bend our ear to the counsel of deceit,
and scoff at what is holy from the seat of pride.

Blessings upon us when we delight in the truth of God,
and ponder God's Law by day and by night,
when we stand up for truth in face of the lie,
when we mouth no slogans and betray no friends.

Then we shall grow like trees planted by streams of water,
that yield their fruit in due season,
whose leaves do not wither.

We struggle with evil in our hearts,
tossed to and fro like chaff in the wind,
a rootless people whose lives have no meaning,
unable to stand when judgment comes,
desolate, outside the house of our God.

May ways of wickedness perish among us:
forgive us, O God, and renew us,
lead us in paths of justice and truth,
obedient to your Wisdom and Will,
trusting in the hope of your promise.

Giver of life, save us from the desert of faithlessness and nourish us with the living water of your Word, that we may bring forth fruit that will last, in the name of Jesus Christ our Saviour.

GOD'S ANOINTED ONE

Refrain: *Come, refining fire of Love.*

WHY do the nations rage at one another?
Why do we plot and conspire?
The powerful of the earth set themselves high,
the people collude with their pride.
We whisper against those God anoints,
chosen to embody God's will.

Do not be mocked and derided, O God:
speak to us in your wrath, terrify us in your fury,
break us with your rod of iron, bring us in fear and trembling
to fall down before you and kiss your feet.

But who *is* this, God's chosen one – God's *Son?*
Inheritor of the earth and all its people?
You take our rage upon yourself,
mocked and crucified, yet meeting all with love.

Ah, Fire that shrivels up our hates,
and brings us to our knees in awe!
Ah, Light that pierces all our fury,
laying bare our greed and pride!
Forgive us, for we know not what we do.

Come, wondrous Ruler of the universe,
holy and just, compassionate and merciful.
Come, universal Reign of peace.
Come, Anointed One, in glory!

Ruler of heaven and earth, raising Jesus from the dead and giving him the victory,
work in us the power of your saving love and bring us to share in your reign;
through Jesus Christ our Saviour.

THE STRUGGLE BETWEEN FEAR AND TRUST

Refrain: *Your steadfast love never fails.*

O GOD, how many are my foes.
They rise up against me,
surrounding me in the night,
adversaries and friends alike,
whispering that you cannot help me.

But you are a shield about me,
you are my glory, and you lift my head high.
I cry to you as I sleep and as I wake,
and the voice of your Presence sustains me.

I am afraid of the powers that prowl within me,
howling in the dark of the moonless night.
I tremble at the thousands and thousands
of weapons and armies swarming around me.
Arise, O God, deliver me: smite them on the cheek,
break their teeth, grind them to the dust.

No, do not destroy them: call out to them,
Rebellious powers, lay down your arms,
return to the God who made you.
Cease your oppression and fury,
and seek the mercies of God.

Liberator, setting us free,
your blessing be upon your people.

*Shield and protector of all, hear the prayers of those who call upon you, and set
them free from violence, persecution, and fear, that all may know the deliverance
that belongs to you alone. We ask this in the name of Jesus our Liberator.*

THE PEACE OF GOD

Refrain: *All manner of thing shall be well.*

ANSWER me when I call, O God
for you are the God of Justice.
You set me free when I was hard-pressed:
be gracious to me now and hear my prayer.

Men and women,
how long will you turn my glory to my shame?
How long will you love what is worthless
and run after lies?

Know that God has shown me such wonderful kindness.
When I call out in prayer, God hears me.

Tremble, admit defeat, and sin no more.
Look deep into your heart before you sleep, and be still.

Bring your gifts, just as you are,
and put your trust in God.

Many are asking, Who can make us content?
The light of your countenance has gone from us, O God.

Yet you have given my heart more gladness
than those whose corn and wine and oil increase.
I lie down in peace and sleep comes at once,
for in you alone, O God, do I dwell unafraid.

*Faithful defender, do not let our hearts be troubled, but fill us with such confidence
and joy that we may sleep in peace and rise in your presence; through Jesus Christ
our Saviour.*

A PRAYER FOR REPENTANCE

Refrain: *Gently turn my face to the sun.*

AT the turning of the day
I make ready for my prayer,
emptying my mind, opening my heart,
my whole self watching and waiting.

Out of the silence comes my cry,
the groaning of my spirit,
profound, beyond words.
O God my Deliverer, listen, and answer.

You take no delight in wickedness:
evil may not sojourn with you.
The boastful may not stand before your eyes,
the proud wither at your glance.
You silence those who speak lies,
you withstand the thrust of the vengeful.

Only through the gift of your steadfast love
do I dare to enter your presence.
I will worship in your holy house
in fear and in trembling.
So easy is it to fall in false ways –
lead me, O God, in your justice,
make my path straight before me.

For there is no truth in our mouths,
our hearts are set on destruction,
our throats are an open sepulchre,
we flatter with our tongue.

Our speeches are honeyed with peace,
smooth words slide from our lips.
The wavelengths dance with lies,
siren songs deceptive in the dark.

Refrain: Gently turn my face to the sun.

Make us feel together the weight of our guilt,
let us fall by the burden of our deceits,
crumbling by reason of our trespass,
lost because of our rebellion.

Pluck us from the despair that follows the lie,
no longer weighed down with the burden of falsehood.
Strengthen our steps in obedience to truth,
turn our lamentation to dancing and joy.
Set us on fire with unquenchable love:
we shall honour your name, exulting with praise.

Blessed be God,
showering blessings on the just and the unjust.
Blessed be God,
enduring with us the showers of black rain.
Blessed be God,
shuddering with pain when sirens wail.
Blessed be God,
our blasts but a feather in the wind of the Spirit.
Blessed be God,
our evil but a drop in the ocean of love.
Blessed be God,
redeeming our wastes and our sorrows.
Blessed be God.

*Source of all justice and goodness, hating deception and evil, lead us in the paths
of truth and godliness, and keep us from all lasting harm. So shall we sing out
our joy in you, O Christ the Living Truth, our Redeemer.*

A DESPERATE CRY IN TIME OF ILLNESS

Refrain: *I cry out to the Void:*
              How long, O God, how long?

HIDEOUS afflictions of a turbulent age –
virus, cancer, thrombosis, ulcer –
warheads in the fluids of my being:
I am caught in a world that is twisted,
trapped in its web of corruption,
tempted to blame my ills on to 'them',
tempted to avoid the hatred within.

Hard pressed by anxiety and discord,
carriers of disease, injectors of poison,
overwhelmed by malice and fear.
Paralysed, depressed, we cannot move,
spun in the vortex of death.

Distressed in the very depths of our being,
bones shaking, cells mutating,
we are almost in despair.

In your mercy and grace set us free.
Refine us in the fire of your love.
Our cry is of hope, yet struggling with doubt,
a stammer gasping for breath in the night.

Turn your face to me, save my life;
deliver me in the endurance of love,
ease the burden of guilt and of pain,
let me know the grace of your presence,
now in this life and through the shades of the grave.

I am weary with my suffering,
every night I flood my bed with tears.
I drench my couch with weeping,
my eyes waste away out of grief,
I grow weak through the weight of oppression.

Refrain: *I cry out to the Void:*
              How long, O God, how long?

You that work evil and seek to destroy,
loosen your grip, away from my presence.
For God has heard the sound of my weeping,
forgives me with delight and lightens my gloom.
The destroyers will be ashamed and sore troubled:
trembling, they will be stripped of their power,
no longer able to harm.

And no, I will not gloat or hate,
in the Love of God I will hold on to you yet.
In the anger and hope of the wrath of our God,
come to the place of repentance and mercy.
And you, silent virus, invisible, malignant,
bound up with my bodily being,
are you an enemy that I can befriend,
or at least contain in a place of your own –
your power to harm taken away,
brought with us to the glory of God?

*God of mercy and tenderness, giver of life and conqueror of death, look upon our
weakness and pain, and bring us to health and to wholeness, that we may sing
a new song to your praise; through Jesus Christ, Redeemer of the powers.*

A SOCIETY IN FRAGMENTS

Refrain: Judge of the world, come and save us.

O GOD, we are shaken by terror,
our hearts grow cold through fear.
The lions roar, their teeth are bared,
they pounce at our throats and tear us apart.

The powers that be stand over us,
whispering treason to workers for peace,
declaring redundant the awkward and angular,
destroying by rumour the worth of a name.

Old loyalties no longer bind us,
family, neighbourhood, union, factory.
The young prowl the streets and the precincts,
alienated, rootless, pain turning to violence.
And the old, the weak, and the poor all cringe,
their welfare, their lives, threatened and vulnerable.

Your will for us, dear God, is sure and steady,
that we do justly, love mercy,
and walk humbly in your Way.
You would not have us return evil for evil,
plundering our enemies and requiting our friends.

Who can stand in your presence
with righteousness and integrity of heart?
Our hearts and our minds conceive evil:
they are pregnant with mischief and bring forth lies.
We dig the pit of our doom,
and fall into the hole we have made.

Our wickedness returns on our head,
we are crushed by the violence we have spawned.
Our lives are trampled to the ground,
our very being spent in the dust.

Refrain: Judge of the world, come and save us.

We cannot but sense your love as your wrath,
Judge of the world come with dread to save us.
Who can stand against the blast of your fury,
fiery shafts sprung from your bow?
Who can bear the anguish and pain in your eyes
as you scour and cleanse us with lasers?

And yet we give you thanks and praise,
for you will not let us go into the Void.
You bear the cost of our redeeming,
the Judge of all the world does right,
bringing us through tears to love for our neighbour,
leading us in pathways to glory and peace.

*Judge and Saviour, pierce the secrets of our hearts and bring to light our hidden
sins. Purify and strengthen us in faith, and give us courage to strive with evil
and bear witness to your just and loving realm. This we pray according to the Way
and in the Name of Jesus Christ our Redeemer.*

STEWARDS OF CREATION

Refrain: *Creator God, Source of all life,*
             how gloriously does your name resound,
             echoing to the bounds of the universe!

THE morning stars sing for joy, and the youngest child cries
    your name.
The weak in the world shame the strong, and silence the
    proud and the rebellious.

When I look at the heavens, even the work of your fingers,
the moon and the stars majestic in their courses –
the eagle riding the air, the dolphin ploughing the sea,
the gazelle leaping the wind, the sheep grazing the fells –
who are we human beings that you keep us in mind,
children, women, and men that you care so much for us?

Yet still you bring us to life, creating us after your image,
stewards of the planet you give as our home.
How awesome a task you entrust to our hands.
How fragile and beautiful is the good earth.

*Creator God, amid the immensities of the universe you seek us out and call us to
be partners in your work of creating. May we not fail you.*

A PRAYER FOR CONCILIATORS

Refrain: *O God, steady our nerve that we may see clearly:*
                strengthen our will in working for peace.

NUCLEAR within and without, we are breaking apart:
cells disintegrating; virus and cancer;
the splitting of atoms; a new black death;
terrorists' dens burrowing the suburbs.

The tired game goes on, the reeds of the world trembling:
pre-emptive strikes; the tactics of bullies;
inaccurate bombings; one cell is blasted.

Hydra-like the desperate multiply:
the smallest of bombs lost in a suitcase:
revenge in mind, no matter who suffers.

Tares and wheat – can you tell them apart?
Neighbour subversive, our own heart corrupt.

International law – not my country right or wrong,
muscle frightened of wasting sickness.
Rational policing – not the sheriff's bully.
Restraining force at a minimum –
not the unleashing of eagle or bear.
Sanctions hurting us – no wonder we're reluctant.
Complexity recognized – simple solutions are final.

Can the powerful admit they have limits?
Give up their arrogance?
Know their own despair?
Understand desperate folk?

Work on in hidden ways, brave conciliators in conflicts:
patriots of earth: allied to no state, not even their own;
loyal to a future not one of us sees;
immaculately suited aliens in the strangest of lands.

Those locked in conflict – do they not see?
they all want their grandchildren
to breathe the good air.

Courage, bomb disposers who delve hearts and minds:
ease the finger from the trigger and button;
defuse the boiling fury, open the eyes blinded with rage.

You will come away wounded, paying a price for us all.
But judgment and mercy: these alone are left now.
We must love one another – or die.

O God of Wisdom, as we pray for those who are burdened with the tasks of negotiation among the peoples of the world, steady our nerves and strengthen our wills, that we may pursue the way of reconciliation among our families and communities, in the Spirit of Jesus Christ who pioneered that way.

DESPAIR AND HOPE IN A DARK TIME

Refrain: How long, O God, how long?

WHAT are they now but a name,
the empires of old that have vanished?
What are they now but ruins,
cities that gleamed with pride?
Where will our idolatry end?
How many more succumb to the engines of war?

Warsaw and Dresden, Geurnica and Hamburg,
Hiroshima, Beirut, and Hanoi –
What fury to come from our darkened hearts?
We hanker after the Abyss,
as we and our cities go into the night.

You that wept for Jerusalem,
that knew not what made for its peace,
see now your prophecy extend
as we enter the eclipse of our God.

We stare dumbly at the death camps of hell:
lo! dark Evil is crowned
in the midst of the tortured and dying.
The needy are forgotten,
the oppressed know not the stronghold of God.

The hope of the weary grows dim;
the heavens are empty;
no ear hears the moan of those stricken down
beneath a pitiless sky.

O God, don't you hear the hard-pressed cries?
Have you forgotten? When will you listen?
How long must we endure, how long?

I can no longer praise you for shattering my enemies,
proud of the justice of my cause.
Nor can I claim you for our side,
and urge you to slay them and blot out their name.
We are snared in the work of our own hands:
our own feet are caught in the net that we hid.

But I will not give in to despair,
for you came to your people of old,
in desert and exile, betrayal and death,
giving joy and great hope,
the light of your Presence
in the least expected of places.

Even from the depths of our doom
comes the cry of the victory of God.
Alleluia! Alleluia!

O God of hope, be with us through the depths of our despair, and work in us the costly ways of peace, that in justice and gentleness your reign may come on earth.

THE PLEADING OF THE POOR

Refrain: Remove the sting of the powerful.

WHY do you stand far off, O God, so mute,
hiding yourself from your people in time of our need?
We are pursued by the arrogant rich:
let them be trapped in the schemes of their devising.

They boast of the desires of their hearts:
greedy for gain, they curse and denounce you.
In the pride of their countenance they no longer seek you,
cold-eyed in denial that there is such a God.

And yet their ways prosper:
loftily making their judgments, they scoff at us.
They think in their hearts they will not be disturbed,
through all generations never meeting adversity.

But their mouths are full of deceit and cursing,
under their tongues are oppression and mischief.
They sit in ambush by the forest road:
in city streets they stalk and murder.
Their eyes watch stealthily for the helpless,
they lurk like lions to seize the poor.

The afflicted are crushed, we sink down and fall
under the weight of their scheming devices.
Denied a name, defrauded of land,
we are reduced to a number,
no voice in our destiny.

The powerful think in their hearts, God has forgotten.
God has turned away and will never see.
O God, cry aloud till they hear you:
disturb their conscience, call them to account.

Forget not the afflicted,
do justice to the oppressed and the orphans.
May the powerful strike terror no more.
Break the strength of their arms,
scour out all wickedness from them.

Hear the desire of the poor,
strengthen our hearts.
May the rich denounce their pride and their greed,
the wickedness that brims with excess.

May they see themselves without their fine clothes,
naked and defenceless before you.
We know that we are their judges, O God,
to purge them with truth and refine them with love,
and together be received in your mercy.

O God, listening and suffering, your silence makes us think you are deaf to our cries: test our faith and patience no more than we can bear, and be known among us as the judge of the earth who does right; through Jesus Christ our Saviour.

THE REPENTANCE OF THE RICH

Refrain: *Melt the ice of our hearts,*
              release the spring of the trap.

In arrogance we rich have pursued the poor:
let us be trapped in the schemes we have devised.
We have boasted of the desires of our hearts:
greedy for gain we have renounced you, O God.

In the pride of our countenance we have not sought you,
cold-eyed in denial we have turned away wilful.
Our ways prospered, our profits increased:
loftily making our judgments, we scoffed at our foes.
We thought in our hearts, We shall not be disturbed,
through all generations not meeting adversity.

Our mouths were full of cursing and scoffing.
Under our tongues were oppression and mischief.
We have sat in ambush in country lanes,
in city streets we have stalked and murdered.
Our eyes have watched stealthily for the helpless,
we lurked like lions to seize the poor.

We crushed the afflicted, they sank down and fell
under the the weight of our frozen hearts.
We denied them a name, defrauded them of land.
We reduced them to a number, no voice in their destiny.
We thought in our hearts, God has forgotten.
God has turned away and will never see.

At last their cry reaches our ears,
we hear the whisper of a conscience revived.
Call us, O God, to account.
Do not forget the ones we afflicted.
Do justice through us to the orphans.

May we strike terror no more.
Break the strength of our arms,
return us to the ways of justice and law.
Hear the desire of the poor:
strengthen their hearts.

We renounce our pride and our greed,
the wickedness that brims with excess.
Defenceless and naked before you,
may we be judged by those we oppressed.
Refine us with fire, purge us with truth,
bring us at last to your mercy.

*O God of light and truth, bring us face to face with our weakness and fear, that
we may be freed to greet the outcast with love, no longer trampling them under
our feet or freezing them out of our hearts. We pray this in the generous laughter
of the Spirit of Jesus Christ.*

THE PRAYER OF A TREMBLING HEART

Refrain: *As a hazelnut lies in the palm of my hand,*
so I rest secure in the presence of God.

I FEAR the fanatics who toy with the trigger,
oiling their rifles with consummate care,
ready to pounce in the dimly lit alley,
raping the makers of peace and of justice.

But to flee like a bird to the mountains –
no safety in the caves of the earth in our day:
the very foundations are splitting apart,
there is nowhere to go but the place where we are.

I turn again in your presence, dear God,
seeking to renew my trust in your care.
For we tremble and shake, gripped by that fear:
the world we have known is crumbling around us,
invisible rain falls on the mountains,
even the caves of the earth fill with rubble.

Within the future that is coming to meet us,
still are you present with us, O God.
Though you seem so remote in our days,
turning your back, dead to the world,
yet we believe that you hold us in mind,
purging us of violence and hardness of heart,
raining coals of fire in our wickedness,
burning up our fury in your own scorching wind.

Give us new integrity of heart,
renew in us the deeds that you love,
justice and mercy, compassion and courage.
Then face to face shall we see you,
knowing and known, loving and loved.

O God of roaring fire and kindly flame, seeking to harness the wild winds of our winter, burning the decayed, and warming new seeds, steady our hearts, deepen our trust, lead us through to the birth of a new age, in Jesus Christ our Pioneer.

WORDS AND THE WORD

Refrain: *O God, fulfil your promise:*
           let your Word take flesh among us.

WHO speaks any longer the truth of the heart,
words that are clear of corruption and lies?
Neighbour speaks false unto neighbour,
flattery on our lips, deceit in our hearts.
The proud, silver-tongued with smooth words,
control the dumb and the awkward of speech.

O God, cut out the forked tongue, silence the lying lips.
Save us from the corruption of language,
from manipulators of words, greedy for power.
For we drown in menacing lies:
the spring of original falsehood now swells to torrent and spate.

May the exiles and migrants, denied their own language,
find living words to shape their own truth,
words that give meaning to lives without purpose,
that heal and inspire and reach deep in the heart.

Speak to us out of your silence, O God,
our minds purged of gossip and chatter.
For you are the fountain of all that is true,
a wellspring deep that never fails.

It is there that we drink long of your Word,
as sure as a friend who is tested and tried.
For your Promise is true and worthy of trust,
like silver refined in the furnace.

Spirit of truth, lead us into all truth, and give us the words to speak it, words that spring deep in the heart and do not distort or betray. We pray this in the name of the One who lived that truth, Jesus Christ our Saviour.

THE PAIN OF THE HEART

Refrain: *Warm the pain of my heart,*
              with the lance of your healing.

How long, O God, how long?
You hide your face from me,
you utterly forget me.

How long, O God, how long?
My being is in anguish and torment,
my heart is grieved day and night.

How long, O God, how long?
Icy death, dread and despair,
insidious foes, they strengthen their grip.

Dull are my eyes and lifeless,
as I stare at the desolate places.
Give light to my eyes,
stir up my will and my passion,
my trust in your life-giving Spirit.

Fill my heart with compassion and strength,
that I may rejoice in your generous love,
able to strive with my foes,
no longer dead in the depths of my being.

Yes, at the moment of emptiness and dread
you surprise me with joy and deliverance.
I will sing and shout with delight,
for you have overwhelmed me with grace.

O living loving God, taking to yourself the pains of the world, cherish our wounded hearts in a tender embrace, and cradle our scars, that we may witness to your glory; through the Pain-bearer Christ we pray.

THE FOLLY OF THE RICH

*Refrain: Fill our hearts with compassion,
           our wills with justice.*

LIKE fools we say in our hearts, "There is no God."
We have become so vile in our deeds
that no one among us does good.

God searches long among the children of earth
. to see if any act wisely,
any who seek to follow the Way.
But we have turned aside from our God,
we are caught in the web of corruption.

There is none that does good, no, not one.
The mists of evil cloud our understanding:
we devour one another like bread,
delighting in the slaughter of peoples:
no longer do we pray to God.
Far from the ways of justice and friendship,
we frustrate the hopes of the poor.

Our hearts will be struck with terror and grief
when we see God saving the poor,
turning their fortune to gladness and joy.

Humble us, O God, our wealth turned to ash;
empty us, that we may be filled with your grace.
Turn our feet into the ways of your justice,
that we may ask forgiveness of those we have wronged.

Then Jacob shall rejoice, and Israel shout for joy,
the whole earth shall sing and be glad,
all the peoples content in their day,
shrivelled seeds warmed by the poor,
the wealthy led at last to the dance.

O God of the poor, prune our lives of all that we cling to. O Spirit of true wealth, draw us through the narrow gate of loss. O Christ who lives in those we neglect, through their generosity turn us to repentance, that we may be forgiven.

FRIENDS OF GOD

Refrain: *Friend of God, deepen your Spirit within us,*
           for you laid down your life for your friends.

DEAR God, who are the honoured guests in your tent?
Who may dwell in your presence upon your holy mountain?
Who may commune with those who are your heart's desire,
lovingly embraced in the union of friends?

Those who lead uncorrupt lives,
and do the thing that is right,
who speak the truth from their hearts,
and have not slandered with their tongue.

Those who have not betrayed their friends,
nor rained down abuse on their neighbours,
in whose eyes the shifty have no honour,
but hold in high esteem those who fear God.

Those who give their word to their neighbour,
and do not go back on their promise,
who have not grown wealthly at the expense of the poor,
nor grown sleek with flattery and bribes.

Those who recognize the outcast as the one whom they need,
who forgive to seventy times seven,
who depend on the mercy of God,
and live the highest law that is love.

Those who are steadfast and kind,
who are resilient and patient and humble,
who know the cost of a morsel of justice,
a glimpse of compassion in times that are savage.

Their roots are deep in the being of God,
their arms are spread wide in welcome embrace.
They are faithful, joyful, and blessed,
God's sisters and brothers and friends.

Loving God, whose name is Friendship, so guide us in your Spirit that we may embrace the way that finds joy in giving all for others, so that even our enemies may become our friends, after the pattern of Jesus of Nazareth who loved his own even to the end.

PRAYER FOR THE DEPARTED

Refrain: Greet them in the joy of your presence.

O GOD our refuge and strength,
preserve us from lasting harm.
Again and again we affirm,
in times both of doubt and of trust,
You are our faithful Creator,
in you alone is our bliss.

We thank you for all your holy people,
all whose lives give you glory.
We praise you for your martyrs and saints,
in whom you take great delight.

As for those held in highest esteem,
those idols adored by the crowd,
those gods they fête and run after,
we will not take their name on our lips.
They are bloated with pride and success,
punctured by thorns in the late autumn wind.

Your name alone do we praise,
our resting place now and for ever.
You feed us with the Bread of Life,
you nourish us with the Cup of Salvation.

We have been so fortunate in our days,
and in the places were we have lived.
To no one else belongs the praise,
but to you, the great Giver of gifts.

We give you thanks for the wisdom of your counsel,
even at night you have instructed our hearts.
In the silence of the darkest of hours
we open our ears to the whisper of your voice.

Refrain: *Greet them in the joy of your presence.*

We have set your face always before us,
in every cell of our being you are there.
As we tremble on the narrowest of paths,
the steadying of your hand gives us courage.
Fleet of foot, with our eyes on the goal,
headlong in the chasm we shall not fall.

Therefore our hearts rejoice and our spirits are glad,
our whole being shall rest secure.
For you will not give us over to the power of death,
nor let your faithful one see the pit.

You will show us the path of life:
in your countenance is the fulness of joy.
From the spring of your heart flow rivers of delight,
a fountain of water that shall never run dry.

*O God of the living, keep our eyes fixed on the goal of our journey, that we may
be fleet of heart, and in all our dyings leap to the embrace of the One who lures us
with love, the pioneer of our salvation, Jesus, our elder brother and faithful friend.*

AN ANGRY CRY FOR JUSTICE

Refrain: *Take the sword, O God, from our hands,*
           wield it with truth and with healing.
    ✔*Let justice roll down like waters,*
           righteousness like an ever-flowing stream.

HEAR my cause, O God, for it is just:
listen to my prayer from lips that do not lie.
Let judgment come forth from your presence:
let your eyes discern what is right.
Though you test me by fire,
and search my heart in the dark of night,
you will find no wickedness in me.
My mouth is not that of the deceiver,
I have kept true to your Word.
My steps have held firm to your paths,
my feet have not stumbled.

I call upon you, O God, for you will answer:
incline your ear to me, and hear my words.
Show me the wonders of your steadfast love,
O Saviour of those who come to you for refuge.
By your right hand you deliver them
from the deadly grip of those who surround them.
Keep me as the apple of an eye,
✔hide me under the shadow of your wings
from the onslaught of the wicked,
from my enemies encircling me to put me in chains.
They have closed their hearts to pity:
their mouths speak pride and arrogance.
They track me down and surround me on every side,
watching how to bring me to the ground.
They are like lions greedy for their prey,
like young lions lurking in ambush.

Refrain: *Take the sword, O God, from our hands,*
              wield it with truth and with healing.
              Let justice roll down like waters,
              righteousness like an ever-flowing stream.

Though I trust I am safe in your presence, O God,
yet do I fear, there is terror in my heart.
Arise, stand in their way and cast them down:
deliver me from the wicked by your sword.
Slay them with your iron fist,
slay them that they perish from the earth,
destroy them from among the living.
May they choke on the grapes of your wrath,
let their bellies be filled with maggots.
May their children never come of age,
their heritage dying with them.
As for me, I shall see your face because my cause is just:
when I awake and see you as you are, I shall be satisfied.

O God, like the psalmist of old I am angry
at the ways of the brutal on earth.
Afraid of their cruelty and greed,
I tremble on the point of their sword.
Yet the hammer of my words and my cries
is held in my hands, poised in the air.
For I know the evil in my own heart,
the lying, the pride, and the arrogance.
Purge me of self-righteousness and hatred,
of smugness and satisfied smile.
Help me to love my enemies with truth,
for we are all children of your love.
Even as I pray for your justice,
for the vindication of your promise,
that oppressors may triumph no more,
that their victims may run free in the wind,
so I pray for my deliverance too.
Save us through judgment and mercy,
dependent as we are on your faithfulness.

O God, compassionate and just, wielder of the one sword that pierces with truth and healing, penetrate the murk and fury of our hearts, that our anger may be shaped by the power of your Spirit, that we may create with you that Commonwealth of Justice and of Peace that is yours alone, and for which we pray through Jesus Christ our Saviour.

RESCUE

Refrain: *Praise to the God of compassion and love,
the power that rescues and saves.*

I LOVE you, O God my strength,
my crag, my fortress, and my deliverer,
the rock to which I cling for refuge,
my shield, my saviour, and my stronghold.
I called to you with loud lamentation,
and you sprang the trap which held me fast.

The waves of death swept over my head,
the floods of chaos surged around me.
The cord of the grave tightened about my neck,
the snares of death sprang shut in my path.
In my anguish I called to you, O God:
I cried in desperation for your help.

Your ear was closer to me than I thought:
you heard me from the depths of my heart.
Then did it seem that the earth was quaking:
the foundations of the hills were shaken:
they trembled because of the power of your anger.

Down you came like a dragon,
swooping on the wings of the wind.
Smoke went forth from your nostrils,
and a consuming fire from your mouth.
You parted the heavens and came down,
riding upon the cherubim,
thick darkness under your feet.
Your voice roared through the heavens,
sharp arrows of lightning,
roll upon roll of thunder,
laying bare the foundations of the world.

Like an eagle you swooped down and took me,
lifting me from the jaws of the sea.
You delivered me from all that imprisoned me,
from those I thought stronger than I.
They fell upon me in the day of calamity,
yet you rescued me and led me to safety.
You brought me into a broad place,
you gave me freedom because you delight in me.

I deserve no reward for anything I have done,
no recompense for the cleanness of my hands.
Have I kept to your ways, O God,
and not turned aside to do evil?
Was my eye always on your command,
did I take your wisdom to my heart?
I dare claim no innocence in your presence,
corrupt have been the deeds of my hands.

Yet still you delight in me – I am astonished –
loving and pursuing the one you are creating,
yearning for me to live in your image.
You are faithful even when I betray you,
when I feel the wrath of your love.
You carefully smooth out my crookedness,
forgiving my sin and wrongdoing.

Such are the faces of your Love,
each reflected in the pool of my being.
For you will save a humble people,
and bring down the high looks of the proud.
You light a lamp for my path,
you make my darkness to be bright.
With your help I can meet all that comes,
with the help of my God I can face evil's defences.

Refrain: *Praise to the God of compassion and love,*
              the power that rescues and saves.

O God, your Way is perfect,
your Word has been tried in the fire.
You are a shield to all who trust in you.
You are my rock and I hold to you.
You gird me with strength
and make my way safe before me.
You make my feet like the feet of the deer,
you set me surefooted on the mountain path.

You teach my hands to fight,
and my arm to aim true with an arrow.
You have given me the shield of salvation;
your right hand guides and supports me.
Your swift response has made me great:
you lengthen my stride beneath me,
and my feet do not slip.

I pursue my enemies and overtake them,
striving till they cease their rebellion.
I fight them till they surrender their arms,
stumbling and falling before me.
Wild in their panic they stagger,
and cry out for mercy and help.
Tempted as I am to be cruel,
to beat them fine as dust in the wind,
to cast them out like the mire of the streets,
yet in your mercy I spare them.
In my struggle with them you deliver me,
and people I had not known become your servants.
Their strength of resistance withers away,
they come trembling from the last of their strongholds.

I cannot ignore the evil in my ways,
however loyal I have been to your covenant.
I cannot deny the good in my enemies,
however hidden and obscured from my sight.
Though I must strive to put an end to their power,
humbly believing that their evil is monstrous –
for no longer do they see their victims as human,
they see only the power of missile and jet –
yet I resist evil means to disarm them,
refusing to treat them as numbers.
O God, renew in us your covenant of peace,
a promise that you gave to all peoples:
desperate is the need of our day.

God lives! God reigns!
Blessed be the rock of my salvation!
Those who set themselves against you have been subdued,
you have set me free from their grip,
delivering me from days of violence and bloodshed.
For this I give you thanks among the people,
and sing praises to your name.
Great love do you show to those whom you care for,
great triumph in fulfilling your purpose of glory,
keeping faith with David your servant,
with his descendants in flesh and in faith.

O Saviour God, lead us through the taut place of our despair, that we may emerge into a land broad and free, through Jesus Christ crucified and risen.

THE LOVE THAT MOVES THE STARS

Refrain: *Praise to the Love that moves the stars,*
                  and stirs in the depths of our hearts.

THE web of the world trembles,
the whisper of a great wind passing.
The caressing of strings makes music,
its sighs reach the ends of the world.

The stars in the heavens chant the glory of God,
pulsing their praise across aeons of space.
From the soft radiance of a summer dawn
to the stormy sunset of a winter's evening,
from the darkest and wildest of mountain nights
to the stillness of moonlit seas,
the voice of praise is never silent,
yet all without speech or language
or sound of any voice.

So too with the mighty sun,
come forth as a bridegroom from his tent,
rejoicing at his wedding day,
exulting in youthful splendour and beauty.
He climbs the sky from the eastern horizon,
he declines to the west at the end of the day,
and nothing can escape the fire of his presence.

Galaxies beyond take up the cry,
suns every more brilliant and huge:
Arcturus twenty times the size of Earth's sun,
Sigma in Dorado hundreds of thousands,
Aldebaran millions of miles in diameter,
Alpha in Lyre three hundred thousand light years away:
all, all proclaim the glory of God.

The law of God is perfect, refreshing the soul,
the words of God are sure, and give wisdom to the simple.
The justice of God is righteous, and rejoices the heart,
the commandment of God is pure, and gives light to the eyes.
The fear of God is clean, and endures for ever,
the judgments of God are true, and just in every way.

So they dance as the stars of the universe,
perfect as the parabolas of comets,
like satellites and planets in their orbits,
reliable and constant in their courses.

The Wisdom of God – more to be desired than gold,
sweeter than syrup and honey from the comb.
And by her is your servant taught,
in the very keeping of her there is great reward.

Who can tell how often I offend?
Cleanse me from my secret faults.
Keep your servant from pride and conceit,
lest they get the dominion over me.
So may I stand in your presence,
innocent of great offence.
Let the words of my mouth
and the meditations of my heart,
be always acceptable in your sight,
O God, my strength and my redeemer.

Creator God, yearning and striving to bring harmony out of chaos, so fill with your Wisdom the inscape of our being, and so move with the Wind of your presence among the landscapes of our world, that the Earth may reflect the glory and wonder of the universe, transfigured in the image of Jesus Christ, at one with you in the cost of creating.

A PRAYER FOR THOSE WHO GOVERN

Refrain: *Give your Spirit of wisdom and justice*
to those who govern and lead.

GOD of Abraham and Sarah, God of our ancestors,
creating among us your realm and your glory,
bless those who rule on the people's behalf,
give them strength in time of our troubles.

Send them the help of your light and your wisdom,
give them support through the prayers of our hearts.
Remember their promise to serve all the people,
take from them their lust for power and for wealth.

Remember our promise to serve others' good,
accept the sacrifice of lives that are broken.
Give to your people the desire of their hearts,
fulfilling within them all that they cherish.

We shout for joy for your blessings towards us,
we lift high the Cross in the name of our God.
For you saved us with the power of unbroken love,
and indeed you fulfil what we deeply desire.

May the rulers of the people acknowledge your name,
serve the common good in the light of your justice.
Some put their trust in weapons of war,
but we shall trust in the power of your name.
They will decay, rust and collapse,
but those strong in God will endure through the days.

May those who lead us trust you, O God.
Give them wisdom to lead through laws that are just.
For you will answer our prayer in the day of our cry,
fulfilling your nature and your own lasting name.

Wise and compassionate One, guide those who bear office in public life, that they
may use their power for the common good, in village, town, and city, in this and
every land; through Jesus Christ our Servant-Lord.

ROYAL PRIESTHOOD

Refrain: *To God be the glory: alleluia!*

It is your royal road, O God,
it is your sovereign way –
to lead in the spirit of service,
to be stewards in your household,
to be guardians one for another,
to guide others in your paths.

As monarchs rejoice in your strength,
so may we exult in your help.
As the sovereign trusts in your faithfulness,
so do we rely on your steadfastness.

You have given us our heart's desire,
even the gift of your justice and wisdom.
You came to meet us with goodly blessings,
and placed crowns of gold on our heads.
We asked you for life and you gave it us,
long days of contentment in your presence.

You have destined even us for glory,
clothing us with splendour and honour.
You have promised us everlasting felicity,
and made us glad with the joy of your presence.

By your light we shall penetrate the dark,
striving till they yield with our enemies.
All that is evil will wither at your coming,
as the chaff is consumed in the fire.
Those who stir malice will be overwhelmed,
their plots of mischief will come to nothing.

No longer will their infection spread through the years,
to the third and the fourth generations.
You will put all their scheming to flight,
stunning them with a glance from your eye.

Refrain: To God be the glory: alleluia!

Be exalted, O God, in your strength,
the power of your love and your truth,
your wisdom and your justice for ever:
we shall sing for joy and praise your name.

*Sovereign of the universe, who has destined even us for glory, with crowns upon
our heads, enable us in your Spirit to serve one another with justice, that none may
be the victim of exploitation and violence, of cruelty and greed; we pray this in
the name of Jesus Christ, the Poor Man of Nazareth.*

WHY? WHY? WHY?

Refrain for Part One: Why, silent God, why?

MY God, my God, why have you forsaken me?
Why are you so far from helping me?
O my God, I howl in the daytime but you do not hear me.
I groan in the watches of the night, but I find no rest.

Yet still you are the holy God whom Israel long has worshipped.
Our ancestors hoped in you, and you rescued them.
They trusted in you, and you delivered them.
They called upon you: you were faithful to your covenant.
They put their trust in you and were not disappointed.

But as for me, I crawl the earth like a worm,
despised by others, an outcast of the people.
All those who see me laugh me to scorn:
they make mouths at me, shaking their heads and saying,
"He threw himself on God for deliverance:
let God rescue him then, if God so delights in him."

You were my midwife, O God, drawing me out of the womb.
I was weak and unknowing, yet you were my hope –
even as I lay close to the breast,
cast upon you from the days of my birth.
From the womb of my mother to the dread of these days,
you have been my God, never letting me go.

Do not desert me, for trouble is hard at hand,
and there is no one to help me.
Wild beasts close in on me, narrow-eyed, greedy and sleek.
They open their mouths and snarl at me, like a ravening and
    roaring lion.

Refrain for Part One: Why, silent God, why?

My strength drains away like water, my bones are out of joint.
My heart also in the midst of my body is even like melting wax.
My mouth is dried up like a potsherd, my tongue cleaves to my
   gums.
My hands and my feet are withered, you lay me down in the
   dust of death.

The huntsmen are all about me:
a circle of wicked men hem me in on every side,
their dogs unleashed to tear me apart.
They have pierced my hands and my feet –
I can count all my bones –
they stand staring and gloating over me.
They divide my garments among them
they cast lots for my clothes.

The tanks of the mighty encircle me,
barbed wire and machine guns surround me.
They have marked my arm with a number,
and never call me by name.
They have stripped me of clothes and of shoes,
and showered me with gas in the chamber of death.

I cry out for morphine but no one hears me.
Pinned down by straitjacket I scream the night through.
I suffocate through panic in the oxygen tent.
Sweating with fear, I await news of my doom.

No one comes near with an unmasked face,
no skin touches mine in a gesture of love.
They draw back in terror, speaking only
in whispers behind doors that are sealed.

Be not far from me, O God: you are my helper, hasten to my aid.
Deliver my very self from the sword, my life from the falling of
   the axe.
Save me from the mouth of the lion,
poor body that I am, from horns of the bull.

Silent God, we bring the cries of our battered hearts, and the cries of those burdened by illness and bowed down by the weight of oppression. We bring them so that we may not be silent. Hear us in the name of Jesus, forsaken on the Cross.

Refrain for Part Two: Even though you slay me,
yet will I trust you.

I WILL declare your name to my friends:
in the midst of the congregation I will praise you.
We stand in awe of you and bow down before you,
we glorify and magnify your name.

For you have not shrunk in loathing
from the suffering in their affliction.
You have not hid your face from them,
but when they called to you, you heard them.

My praise is of you in the great congregation,
my vows I will perform in their sight.
We shall praise you with thanksgiving and wonder.
We shall share what we have with the poor:
they shall eat and be satisfied,
a new people, yet to be born.
Those who seek you shall be found by you:
they will be in good heart for ever.

So shall my life be preserved in your sight,
and my children shall worship you:
they shall tell of you to generations yet to come:
to a people yet to be born
they shall declare your righteousness,
that you have brought these things to fulfilment.

So let all the ends of the world remember
and turn again to their God.
Let all the families of the nations worship their Creator.
For all dominion belongs to you,
and you are the ruler of the peoples.

O God of enduring love, whom the clouds obscure, may our eye of faith turn
steadily towards you, patiently waiting in hope for the fulness of your salvation,
bearing the pain of evil days, in Jesus of the Cross, who loved his own even to the
end, and who kept on trusting even when there was no answer to his cry.

Refrain for Part Three: *We trust in the folly of the Cross.*

CAN we now hold on to such faith?
Has the name of God become an offence to our ears?
Is God deaf to the cry of the child,
offering no relief to the burning of pain,
letting the horror of life run wild,
sitting lofty and high, refusing to act?

So do we argue and wrestle in faith,
fiercely refusing to loosen our hold.
We demand that you listen to whisper and howl,
that your deeds may fulfil your nature and name.

This is our story from Jeremiah and Job,
from all who find you obscure and perplexing.
Who are you? Who do you say that you are?
Why must we be buffeted by malice and chance?

Is our cry no more than our pride?
Is our mind too small? Is our eye too dim?
Do not quiet our pain with dazzling display.
The open wound of the child accuses you still.

Is there a cry in the depths of your being,
in the heart and soul of your chosen Christ-Self?
Stretched between earth and the heavens,
we see a striving so awesome,
a strange and harrowing love,
a bearing of pain between father and son,
a loving right through to the end,
through the worst of devil and death.

Truly you are an offence, O God,
and scandalous too are the outcries of faith.
They bite deep into the lines of our faces,
as we strive to be faithful and true.
Keep us from the scandal of hypocrisy,
selfish and faithless, prayers merely mouthed,
so far from the Place of the Skull,
too indifferent to be in conflict with you,
too icily cold for your friendship.

Refrain for Part Three: *We trust in the folly of the Cross.*

Today if you hear the voice of *this* God,
your heart need no longer be hardened.

O God of the Cross, keep us passionate through our wrestling with your ways, and keep us humble before the mystery of your great love, known to us in the face of Jesus Christ.

Refrain for Part Four: *In the depths of our darkness*
you are rising, O Christ.

AND can those who are buried give you worship,
those ground to the dust give you praise?
Will nothing be left but the wind and the silence,
a dead earth, abandoned, forgotten?

But you are a God who creates out of nothing,
you are a God who raises the dead,
you are a God who redeems what is lost,
you are a God who fashions new beauty,
striving with the weight of your glory,
bearing the infinite pain.

The footfalls of faith may drag through our days,
God's gift of a costly and infinite enduring.
We remember your deliverance of your people of old,
we remember the abundance of the earth you have given us,
we remember the care and compassion of folk,
we remember your victory of long-suffering love.

The power of the powers is but a feather in the wind!
Death is transfigured to glory for ever!

*Risen Christ, breaking the bonds of death, shine on us with eyes of compassion
and glory. Let light flood the dungeons of our rejected and downtrodden selves.
So may the oppressed go free, the weak rise up in strength, and the hungry be fed,
now in these our days.*

THE SHEPHERD AND THE HOST

Refrain: *Dwell in me that I may dwell in you.*

DEAR God, you sustain me and feed me:
like a shepherd you guide me.
You lead me to an oasis of green,
to lie down by restful waters.

Quenching my thirst, you restore my life:
renewed and refreshed, I follow you,
a journey on the narrowest of paths.
You keep me true to your name.

Even when cliffs loom out of the mist,
my step is steady because of my trust.
Even when I go through the deepest valley,
with the shadow of darkness and death,
I will fear no evil or harm.
For you are with me to give me strength,
your crook, your staff, at my side.

Even in the midst of my troubles,
with the murmurs of those who disturb me,
I know I can feast in your presence.

You spread a banquet before me,
you anoint my head with oil,
you stoop to wash my feet,
you fill my cup to the brim.

Your loving kindness and mercy
will meet me every day of my life.
By your Spirit you dwell within me,
and in the whole world around me,
and I shall abide in your house,
content in your presence for ever.

Wise and loving Shepherd, you guide your people in the ways of your truth, leading us through the waters of baptism and nourishing us with the food of eternal life: keep us in your mercy, and so guide us through the perils of evil and death, that we may know your joy at the heart of all things, both now and for ever.

THE GLORY OF GOD

Refrain: *Praise to the Glory of God,*
              shining through Jesus Christ.

DEAR God, you are creating the earth and all that is in it,
the whole round world and all who dwell on land or sea.
You have founded life upon the waters,
and drawn it forth from the mysterious deeps.

Who shall climb the mountain of God?
Who shall stand in the holy place?
Those who have clean hands and pure hearts,
who have not set their minds on falsehood,
nor sworn to deceive their neighbours.
They shall receive a blessing from God,
and justice from the God of their salvation.
Such is the fortune of those who draw near their Creator,
who seek the face of the God of Jacob.

Let the gates be opened, let the doors be lifted high,
that the great procession may come in.
Who is the One clothed with glory?
It is our God, the God who has triumphed,
who has striven with evil and prevailed.

Let the gates be opened, let the doors be lifted high,
that the great procession may come in.
Who is the One clothed with glory?
It is the great God of all the universe,
glorious in a Love that never fails.

*May the light and love of God shine in our hearts and through the universe that
the whole creation may be transfigured to glory, in and through Jesus Christ,
radiant in the splendour of the wounds of love.*

A PRAYER OF THE LONELY

Refrain: *You are the source of my faith,*
                you are the goal of my hope.

O GOD, the foundation of my hope,
you are the gound of my trust.
May I not be disappointed in my days,
may the powers of oppression fade away.

Let none who wait for your coming
turn away with empty hands.
But let those who break faith
be confounded and gain nothing.

Show me your ways, O God,
and teach me your paths.
Lead me in your truth and guide me,
for you are the God of my salvation.

I have hoped in you all the day long,
because of your goodness and faithfulness,
your steadfast love to your people,
streaming towards us from days of old.

Remember not the sins of my youth,
nor my trespass and trampling on others.
According to your mercy think on me,
call to mind your agelong compassion.

You are full of justice and grace:
you guide sinners in the Way.
You lead the humble to do what is right,
filled with the gentle strength of the meek.
All your paths are faithful and true,
for those who are loyal to your covenant.

For your name's sake, O God,
be merciful to me, for my sin is great.
I come to you in trembling and awe:
guide me in the way I should choose.

Refrain: *You are the source of my faith,*
              you are the goal of my hope.

I shall be at home with what is right,
I shall dwell at ease in the land.
My children shall be stewards after me,
your creation cared for in days yet to come.
Your friendship is your gift to me,
revealed in the keeping of your covenant.

My eyes look towards you, O God,
and you free me from the snares of the net.
Turn your face to me –
it is full of your grace and your love.

For I am lonely and in misery,
my heart is in pain and constricted:
the arteries of affection are hardened.
Open me wide and lift my heart high,
the breath of your Spirit filling my lungs.
Take to yourself my wretched affliction,
bring me out of my distress,
and forgive me all my sins.

See how strong are the powers of oppression,
eyes full of hatred and violence.
Guard my life and deliver me,
clothe me with integrity and love.

Bring me to the innocence that no longer harms,
for you are my strength and salvation.
I wait for you: you are my hope;
may I never shrink away in shame.

Compassionate and loving God, take from me the burden of self-hatred, the whisper of loathing that says I am worthless. Fill me with the spirit of forgiveness and grace, that I may deeply accept that I am accepted just as I am, in Jesus Christ the Beloved of your Heart.

INNOCENT OR GUILTY?

Refrain for Part One: *We give you thanks, O God,*
                          for you make your people righteous.

GIVE judgment for me, O God,
for I have walked in my integrity,
I have trusted you without wavering.

Put me to the test and try me,
examine my mind and my heart.
For your steadfast love is before my eyes,
and I have walked in your truth.

I have not sat with deceivers,
nor consorted with hypocrites;
I hate the company of evildoers,
and I will not sit with the wicked.

I wash my hands in innocence, O God,
that I may approach your altar,
lifting up the voice of thanksgiving,
and telling of all your marvellous deeds.

Dear God, I love the house of your dwelling,
the place where your glory shines.
Do not sweep me away with sinners,
nor my life with people of blood,
who murder with their evil weapons,
and whose hands are full of bribes.

As for me I walk in my integrity:
redeem me and be gracious to me.
My foot stands on firm ground:
I will bless you in the great congregation.

Refrain for Part Two: Kyrie eleison
                           Christe eleison
                           Kyrie eleison

WHO in this world of ours now
dare take that prayer as their own?
Perhaps the ones imprisoned for conscience,
persecuted and tortured for faith,
tempted to renounce their beliefs,
holding firm to the most sacred of vows.
Yet even the greatest of saints
knows no boast in the presence of God.

Forgive the boast of your people, O God,
self-righteous and blind in our mouthings.
We have not done a tenth of these things,
nor dare we plead any innocence.
We project the evil of our hearts on to others,
and destroy our enemies in your cause.
The drumbeat of the psalmist has sounded
through years of inquisitions and wars.

*We pray for the enemy, in others and in ourselves, the one who whispers the lie
and imprisons the tellers of truth. O God, forgive our laziness, our fear, our
stupidity, and shed on us the painful healing beams of the light of Jesus Christ
the living Truth.*

COURAGEOUS FAITH IN TURBULENT TIMES

Refrain: *In time of disquiet and trouble,*
with courage will I trust you, O God.

GOD is my light and my salvation:
whom then shall I fear?
God is the strength of my life:
of whom then shall I be afraid?
In God alone do I put my trust:
how then can others harm me?

When the wicked, even my enemies,
come upon me to devour me,
they stumble and fall back.
When a mighty army is laid against me,
my heart shall not be afraid.
When war rises up against me,
yet will I put my trust in God.

One thing have I desired of God
that I will seek after,
even that I may dwell in the house of my God
all the days of my life,
to feast my eyes on the beauty of my Creator,
to ponder deeply the gracious will of my God.

In the time of my trouble
you will hide me in your shelter;
in the shadow of your tent
you will conceal me
from those who pursue me;
high on a pinnacle of rock
you will place me safe
from those who surge around me.

Therefore I will offer in your dwelling place
gifts with great gladness:
I will sing and praise your name.

Refrain: *In time of disquiet and trouble,*
               with courage will I trust you, O God.

Listen to me, O God, when I cry to you:
have mercy upon me and be gracious to me.
Do not hide your face from me,
nor cast your servant away in your anger.

The voice of my heart has impelled me:
Seek the face of the living God.
Out of the darkness I discern your presence
in the face of the Risen Christ,
revealing your pain and your joy
in new and abundant life.

Indeed you have been my helper,
you have not forsaken me, O God of my salvation.
Though my family and friends may desert me,
you will sustain me in the power of the Risen One.

Guide me in your way and lead me on your path.
So in the joy of your presence I can meet my adversaries,
even when false witnesses rise up against me,
or those who do me violence and wrong.

I should have utterly fainted but that I truly believe
I shall see your goodness in the land of the living.
I shall patiently wait for your good time:
I put my trust in our faithful Creator:
I shall be strong and let my heart take courage.

In all these things we are more than conquerors
through Christ who loved us.
For I am sure that neither death nor life,
nor angels nor principalities nor powers,
nor things present nor things to come,
nor height nor depth, nor anything else in all creation,
will be able to separate us from the love of God
in Christ Jesus our Servant-Lord and our Saviour.

Creator God, faithful to your covenant with the earth, steady our hearts and wills in these times of great turbulence, that we may in deed fulfil your purpose for us as heralds of your just and lasting peace; through Jesus Christ our Saviour.

THE SILENCE AND THE VOICE

Refrain: *Come, Wind of the Spirit,*
                   with the Voice of our God.

DEAR God, are you the Friend I can trust?
You seem so deaf to my prayer,
to the urgent sound of my voice.
Do you not hear, do you turn away silent,
when I cry out for help?
I lift up my hands in the holy place,
but still I hear no answer.

Let me pause and remember
the holy ground of your presence –
the bush burning with light
at the moment of despair.

You are here in the ones I ignore:
the shuffling old man in the street,
the hollow-eyed woman unkempt,
the neighbour I pass hurriedly by.

I see neither their need nor mine,
it is I who turn silent away.
I collude with the ways of wickedness,
speaking peace with my lips,
unaware of the mischief of my heart.
No wonder I do not hear your voice.
I turn away from your presence,
pulled down by my selfish desires.

Open our eyes that we may see,
unblock our ears that we may hear.
Send us the fury of the desert wind,
or the gentle breeze through the trees.
Whether by shouting or whisper,
face us with dark truths of our ways.

No reward dare we claim,
no generosity from your heart.
No wonder we fall in the midst of our devices,
to be built up in strength no more.

And yet there are times of our passion,
our anger at the traps of the poor,
of those without power or numbers.
The voice of the voiceless is heard in our land,
and the sound of your rejoicing, O God.
You are the strength of our hands
as we strive with the powers for your truth.
Our hearts trust you and we thank you,
we dance for joy and with songs give you praise.

Save your people, bless your heritage,
be our shepherd and guard us.
Protect us and bear with us,
both now and for ever.

Remove from our hearts, O God, our apathy and fear, and give us the Spirit of love and freedom, that we may give passionately of ourselves in companionship with the poor and oppressed, and so serve your just and holy rule, revealed to us in Jesus Christ our Liberator.

AWE IN THE PRESENCE OF POWER

*Refrain: Giving voice to the cry of creation,
              we shout Glory to God in the Highest.*

LET all the powers of the universe praise the Creator,
ascribing to God glory and strength.
In the beauty of holiness we worship you, O God,
giving you the honour due to your name.

Your voice rolls over the waters,
your glory thunders over the oceans.
Your voice resounds through the mountains,
echoing glory and splendour.

Your voice splits even the cedar trees,
breaking in pieces the cedars of Lebanon.
The trees of the mountainside howl in your wind,
uprooted like matchsticks in the roar of your passing.

Your voice divides the lightning flash,
flames of fire come from your tongue.
Your voice whirls the sands of the desert,
the whistling sands of the desert storm.

Your voice makes the oaks shake and shudder,
and strips the forest bare,
and all in your presence cry, Glory!

O God, more powerful than tempest and flood,
reigning over all your creation,
stillness in the eye of the storm,
give strength to your people in awe of you,
give your people the blessing of peace.

*Awesome God, your Love embraces all the powers of creation, and in the presence
of Love we need never be afraid. Give us steadiness and courage and skill to strive
with the energies you have placed in our hands, that the wise use of heat and light,
of atom and laser, may enable the earth and its peoples to flourish and prosper,
according to your will shown to us in Jesus Christ, true image of you, our Creator.*

THE TWO CONVERSIONS

Refrain for Part One: *With gentle hand you raise me,*
                            from death you call me to life.

FROM the depths of despair I cried out,
seared with pain and with grief.
Where are you, O God?
How long must I suffer?

You drew me up from the deeps,
like a prisoner out of a dungeon,
a flesh-body touched by your hand,
flickering and trembling with life.

You brought me out of a land full of gloom,
a place of hollow silence and cold.
You melted my paralyzed fear:
the warmth of your Sun coursed through my veins.

The wrath of your Love lasts but a moment,
for a lifetime your mercy and healing.
Heaviness and weeping last through the night,
yet day breaks into singing and joy.

I will praise you, O God,
for you have made me whole.
I will give you thanks
in the midst of your people.

Refrain for Part Two: *When my feet stumble and stray,*
your hand steadies and guides me.

IN the strength you gave me I felt secure,
built upon rock, firm as the hills.
Basking in the warmth of your favour,
the prosperity of my days increased.

I slipped into the worship of money,
the goods of this world ensnaring me.
They gathered like a turbulent cloud,
blotting out the sight of your face.

Then I was greatly dismayed,
feeling foolish in toppling pride,
unable to praise you from the wasteland of hell,
to proclaim your name from the graveyards of death.

O God, have mercy upon me,
forgive my self-satisfied pride,
disentangle the web I have woven,
patiently probe me with the scalpel of truth.

You turn my lamentation into dancing,
lifting me to my feet, clothing me with joy.
In the depths of my being I explode into laughter,
and sing with gratitude the triumph of Love.

*Living Christ, look on us with eyes of compassion; call us with the word of
forgiveness, again and again, to seventy times seven, that we may at last hear and
see, and turn our stricken and wounded faces, and know ourselves accepted and
embraced, loved beyond measure and without reserve.*

A PRAYER FOR DELIVERANCE

Refrain: In the midst of struggle and pain
we trust in the Love that endures.

I AM bowed down by the heat of battle;
exhausted I limp back to my tent.
Here is my shelter, my refuge,
the place where I know God is with me.
Deliver me, rescue me, redeem me,
for you are just, and swift to save.
You are a stream of refreshment, an oasis of shade;
you give me manna in the wilderness, ever drawing me on.

Lead me and guide me for the sake of your name:
deliver me out of the nets that entangle me,
for you alone are my strength.
Into your hands I cast my whole being,
knowing that you will redeem me,
O God of salvation and truth.

I hate those who cling to vain idols,
for my trust is in you, living God.
I will be glad and rejoice in your love,
for you have seen my affliction,
and soothed my distress.
You have not abandoned me to the power of my enemy:
you have set my feet in a broad place,
where I may walk at liberty.

Have mercy on me, O God,
for I am distressed and in pain:
no one hears the cry of my loneliness.
My eyes have become dimmed with grief,
the whole of me body and soul.

My life is worn away with sorrow,
and my years with mourning.
My strength fails me because of my affliction,
and my bones are wasting away.

Refrain: *In the midst of struggle and pain*
              we trust in the Love that endures.

I am the scorn of all my enemies,
and a burden to my neighbours.
My acquaintances, they are afraid of me,
shrinking away from my sight.

I am clean forgotten,
like a dead man out of mind.
I have become like a broken vessel.
For I hear the conspiring of many,
the whispering of threats on every side,
as they plot to take away my life.

The hope of my days is in your hands:
I trust you, my God, Thou that art Thou.
Deliver me from the power of my enemies,
from the grip of those who persecute me.
Show your servant the light of your countenance,
and save me in your steadfast love.

Let me not be confounded, O God,
for I have called upon your name.
Let all ungodliness be put to confusion,
and brought to silence in the grave.
Let lying lips be made dumb,
the voices of cruelty and pride
that speak with spite against the just.

How great is your goodness towards us,
poured out on the just and the unjust,
saving us from whisperings within,
from the betrayals of hearts that are frightened,
sheltering us in your refuge
from the strife of tongues.

O God, I give you thanks
for you have shown me marvellous great kindness.
When I was alarmed, like a city besieged,
I felt cut off from your sight.
Nevertheless, you heard the voice of my prayer,
when I cried to you for help.

All your servants love you, O God,
for you enfold us in your faithfulness,
and retrieve us sternly when we are proud.
With firmness of will and courage of heart,
we will follow your way,
trusting that you are our God,
our faithful Creator and Friend.

*Living God, faithful to your covenants, loyal to your people, deepen our trust in
your loving purposes for all humankind, that we may come to no lasting harm.
We pray this in and through Jesus Christ our Redeemer.*

RELEASE FROM THE BURDEN OF SIN

Refrain: *Lift my burdens from my shoulders,*
              for the yoke of your Love is light.

BLESSED are those whose sin is forgiven,
the trace of whose trespass is erased.
Blessed are those whom God does not blame,
in whose heart is no guile.

I kept my secret sins to myself,
I refused to bring them to the light.
My energy wasted away,
my days were full of complaint,
a grumble murmuring in my ears.
Day and night your hand was heavy upon me:
the flow of my being became sluggish and dry,
like parched land in the drought of summer.

Then I acknowledged my sin in your presence:
I hid no longer from myself or from you.
I said, ''I will confess my evil to God.''
So you released me from the guilt of my sin.

For this cause all those who are faithful
pray in their hearts in the day of their troubles.
Even in times of overwhelming distress,
with the thunder and force of waters in flood,
your grace is for me like a temple of rock,
standing firm in the face of the powers,
ordering the discord and chaos within,
preserving my life from utter destruction.
In the eye of the storm I hear the whisper of mercy,
the peace of those who are completely forgiven.

"I will instruct you and guide you,
I will teach you the way you should go.
I will counsel you with my ear to the Truth,
a keen and kindly eye fixed upon you.
Do not be like horse or mule, with no understanding,
whose course must be curbed with bridle and bit."

Many are the pangs of the wicked:
steadfast love surrounds those who trust God.
People of integrity, rejoice in God and be glad:
shout for joy all you that are true of heart.

Compassionate Friend, warm the frozen places of my fear, irrigate the deserts of my apathy, dismantle the wall around my pain and love, lift the burdens of my past, that I may be free to live in the joy of the Risen Christ.

THE GOD OF CREATION AND HISTORY

Refrain: *Praise to the Love that moves the stars*
and stirs the heart of the people.

LET those who serve you praise you, O God,
let the true of heart give you thanks.
Let the melodies of the strings be played,
accompanying our words in your praise.

For your Word, O God, is true,
your deeds reflect your covenant.
You love the justice of relationships made right,
the world is full of your steadfast love.

O God, you are the God of creation:
by your word was the universe made,
the numberless stars by the breath of your mouth.
You held the waters of the seas in the hollow of your hand,
you gathered to yourself all the treasures of the deep.

Let the whole earth be in awe of you,
all the inhabitants of the world greet you with joy.
For you spoke, and the wonderful deed was done;
you commanded, and it all came to pass.

O God, you are the God of history:
all the ways of the nations are but nothing in your sight.
You frustrate the devices of the peoples,
and your counsel and truth stand for ever,
the purpose of your heart to all generations.
Blessed are the people who put their trust in you,
whom you have chosen to serve a high destiny.

Not one of the children of earth can escape you;
all the inhabitants of the earth are in your sight.
You fashion all our hearts
and comprehend all our ways.

A ruler is not saved by a mighty army,
a warrior is not delivered by much strength.
A war horse is a vain hope for victory,
and by its great might it cannot save.
But your eye, O God, is on those who fear you,
who trust in your unfailing love.
You deliver them from the pangs of death,
and feed them in the time of famine.

We wait for you eagerly, O God,
for you are our hope and our shield.
Surely our hearts shall rejoice in you,
for we have trusted in your holy name.
Let your merciful kindness be upon us,
even as our hope is in you.

*O Love, moving the sun and the moon and the stars, weave the pattern of glory
to the bounds of the universe, even the cells of our being.*

GOD THE BEARER OF PAIN

Refrain: *With the strings that are taut with pain*
             compose new music of joy.

WE will bless you, O God, at all times,
your praise opening our lips.
We will exalt your name alone:
the afflicted will hear and be glad.
We give the Pain-bearer thanks:
we magnify the name of our God.

I sought your help and you answered,
you freed me from all my fears.
We look towards you and are radiant:
our faces shall not be ashamed.

The cry of the poor reaches your ears,
you saved us out of our trouble.
Your angel guards and protects us,
bringing your deliverance near.

So do we taste and see
how gracious and good is our God.
You meet us in the depth of our pain,
those who love you and fear you lack nothing.

Come, my children, listen to me:
I will teach you the way of our God.
Who among you relishes life,
wants time to enjoy good things?
Let no spite defile your tongue,
no lies fall from your lips.
Renounce the ways of evil,
pursue peace with all your heart.

Your eyes, O God, turn to the humble poor,
your ears to the cry of the needy and just.
You set your face against those who do wrong,
cutting off the memory of their deeds.

When those who do no harm cry for help,
you come close to their anguish and calm them.
Gently you embrace the broken in heart,
and revive the crushed in spirit.

Many are the afflictions of those who seek good,
but the pain-bearing God is with them.
You penetrate the heart of their suffering,
that they come to no lasting harm.

Evil rebounds on itself,
those consumed with hatred come to nothing.
O God, you redeem the life of your servants:
close to you, they will not be destroyed.

*Pain-bearer God, in our affliction we sense your presence, moving with our
sufferings to redeem them, bringing joy out of tragedy, creating such music as the
world has not yet heard. We praise you with great praise.*

[handwritten margin note, partly illegible: "there is a longing in the heart to reach for you ..."]

[handwritten note: "Peace, Comfort, Assurance ... held in God's hands"]

THE QUIET IN THE LAND

Refrain: *Praise God who delivers the weak from the strong,*
the needy from those who despoil them.

I AM angry at the proud and self-righteous,
yet I see their face in my own.
I wreak havoc in the lives of my neighbours,
seemingly concerned for the good of their souls.
By innuendo I slander a name,
prejudging the ones I dislike,
gossiping in pubs and in churches,
hypocritically enjoying the headlines.

Let us be put to shame and dishonour,
hawks that seek the destruction of life.
Let us be turned back and confounded,
who devise evil against our neighbours.
Let us be like chaff before the wind,
the angel of God driving us on.
Let our way be dark and slippery,
the hound of God pursuing us.
Let the nets of our devising ensnare us,
let us fall to ruin in them,
swallowed up in the pit we dug for others,
for the poor, the defenceless, the oppressed. . .

At such a turn in the world's affairs
the oppressed shall rejoice in the deliverance of God.
From the depth of their being they shall say,
Praise God who delivers the weak from the strong,
the needy from those who despoil them. . .

Malicious witnesses rise up,
spinning traps with their words,
making the innocent sign confessions
about things they know nothing of.
All that is good is called evil;
even if heard the truth is not known.

And yet I prayed for my enemies,
lost in bewildered confusion.
Crumpled with grief I prayed long
as if mourning a companion or brother.
My eyes looked to the ground
as if I were lamenting my mother.

But when I stumbled they laughed me to scorn
and gathered together against me.
As though I were a stranger I never knew
they slandered me without ceasing.
When I slipped they mocked me more and more,
and hissed at me through their teeth . . .

How long, O God, will you look from afar?
Rescue me from the grip of their teeth,
my life from the tearing of lions.
And I will give you thanks in the great congregation,
in the throng of the people I will praise you.

Let not the malicious triumph over their victims,
let not the mockers hate others with their eyes.
For they speak not words that make for peace,
but invent lies against those who are quiet in the
land.

They stretch their mouths to jeer,
they rub their hands with glee,
sweeping the poor off their parcel of land,
claiming – As far as you can see, all is mine . . .

And you also have seen, O God:
do not be silent and hidden away.
Stir yourself, be awake for justice,
for the cause of the poor and oppressed.
Judge us in your righteousness,
let not the proud triumph,
let them not say, "Good, we have our heart's desire;"
let them not say, "Good, we have destroyed them."

Refrain: Praise God who delivers the weak from the strong,
              the needy from those who despoil them.

Let those who rejoice at others' hurt
be completely disgraced and confounded.
Let them be clothed with shame and dishonour
who trample the face of the needy,
exalting themselves at the expense of the poor.
But let those who long for justice
shout for joy and be glad:
let them say, "Great is God!
You delight in all those who serve you."
Then my tongue shall speak of your righteous ways,
and of your praise all the day long.

*Disarm the mighty, O God, and calm their fears. Let scales fall from their eyes,
let them weep tears of repentance, that they may see their enemies as human beings,
and come to know them as the only friends who bear the gift of their salvation,
in Jesus, powerless and victorious in love for us.*

THE JUDGE WHO DOES RIGHT

Refrain: *Pierce to the heart of our wickedness,*
              abandon us not to our doom.

TRANSGRESSION whispers to the wicked, deep in their hearts:
there is no fear of God in their eyes.
They flatter themselves with their own reflection,
imagining their wickedness is a secret for ever.

The words of their mouths are mischief and deceit:
they have ceased to act wisely and never do good.
Lying awake in the night, plotting with malice,
they set themselves on a path that is crooked,
no longer aware of the evil they do.

Your steadfast love, O God, extends through the universe,
your faithfulness to the furthest stars.
Your justice is like the high mountains,
your judgment as the great deep.

So the Judge of all the earth will do right.
You will save us, frail children of the dust:
precious indeed is your kindness and love.
The children of earth find refuge in your shade,
you entertain them to a feast in your house.
You give them water to drink from the river of delight:
for with you is the well of life,
and in your light do we see light.

Continue your goodness to those who know you,
your saving ways to the true of heart.
Let not the foot of the proud trample us,
nor the hand of the arrogant push us aside.
Under the weight of their scheming may they crumple,
their will to do evil extinguished for ever.

O God, wise and discerning in all that you do, deliver us from the illusion that we are better than others; rather than condemning one another, may we come together and kneel in humility, knowing only your mercy and truth, in Jesus Christ our Saviour.

DOGGED TRUST IN GOD

Refrain: *In meeting the powers of evil*
                 let us deepen our trust in God.

Do not fret yourself because of the ungodly,
do not be envious of those who do evil.
For then you become as one of them,
putting yourself in the wrong.
They will soon fade away like grass,
withering like the leaves in drought.
Simply trust in God, and do good:
we shall dwell in the land and graze safely.

Let us delight in your company, O God,
and you will give us our heart's desire.
Let us commit our lives to your goodness,
let us cast all our cares on your shoulders.
Let us trust you to act with justice,
to deliver us in your own good time.
You will make our vindication shine clear as the light,
our integrity bright as the noonday sun.

Let us be still and wait for you patiently,
bearing the tension that all is not well,
calming the restless desire to be certain,
in advance of the day of your coming.
Let us not be vexed when others prosper,
when they weave their evil designs.
May we let go of anger and rage,
refusing to let envy move us to evil.

For the wicked shall be cut down:
those who wait for God shall inherit the land.
In a while the ungodly shall be no more:
we shall look for them in their place:
we shall find it deserted, left to the wind.
The humiliated shall inherit the earth,
they shall enjoy the abundance of peace.

Refrain: In meeting the powers of evil
              let us deepen our trust in God.

The ungodly plot against the righteous
and gnash at them with their teeth.
But you, O God, will laugh them to scorn,
for you know their overthrow comes soon.

The ungodly have drawn the sword from the sheath,
they have aimed their arrows at the poor and the needy,
slaughtering those who walk in truth.
Their swords shall pierce their own hearts,
their arrows and bows shall be broken.
Sin turns in on itself,
and destroys the works of the wicked.

Though the righteous have but a little,
it is better than the hoards of the wicked.
The strong arm of the ungodly shall be broken:
God upholds those who are true of heart.

God cares for the lives of the humble poor,
and their heritage shall be theirs for ever.
They shall not be put to shame in evil days,
but in time of famine they shall eat their fill.
As for the ungodly they shall perish,
they are the enemies of God:
like fuel in a furnace they will be consumed,
like smoke they will vanish away.

The ungodly borrow but never repay:
but the poor are often generous and give.
Those who are blessed by God will inherit the land,
those whom God has cursed will be cut down.
If our steps are guided by God,
and if we delight in God's way,
though we stumble we shall not fall headlong,
for you, O God, will steady us with your hand.

I have been young and now I am old,
but I never saw the good man forsaken,
or his children begging their bread.
The righteous are gracious and lend,
and their children shall be blessed in the land.
Turn from evil and do good,
and you will dwell in the land for ever.
For you, O God, love what is just,
you will not forsake those who are faithful.
But the ways of the unjust will perish for ever,
the seed of the ungodly will be destroyed.

The righteous will inherit the land,
and they will dwell in it for ever.
The mouths of the just utter wisdom,
and their tongues speak what is right.
The law of God is in their hearts,
and their footsteps will not slip.
The ungodly watch out for the righteous,
and seek occasion to slay them.
But God will not abandon them to their power,
nor let them be condemned when they are judged.

We wait for you, O God, and we hold to your Way,
and you will raise us up to inherit the land,
to see the ungodly when they wither away.
I have seen the wicked in terrifying power,
spreading themselves like luxuriant trees.
I passed by again and they were gone,
I searched for them but they could not be found.

Observe the blameless and consider the upright,
for people of peace will have prosperity.
Deliverance for the righteous will come:
O God, you will save them in the time of trouble.

Refrain: In meeting the powers of evil
let us deepen our trust in God.

Enable us in these our days,
we who are the privileged few,
help us to lend our strength to the weak,
our voices to the small and the voiceless.
Help us to sound our compassion and anger,
to strive with those who oppress the downtrodden,
showing them their greed and malice and fear,
helping them to face their enemy within,
that they may open their hearts to be generous.
May they do the same for those they exploit,
that their wickedness too may vanish away.
Together redeem us, long-suffering God,
bring us all to share in your peace.

Be with us, O God, as we struggle for a more just world, yet remind us that our actions so often tighten the mesh that binds the oppressed. Keep us from pride in our own strength, and keep us from despair when evil seems entrenched. Renew our trust in your good purposes for us all. Give us the gift of discernment, that we may know when to strive in the power of your Spirit, and when to be still and wait for your deliverance. Come in your good time, but come soon!

A CRY FROM THE MIDST OF PAIN AND GUILT

Refrain: *From the power of guilt and pain*
             save me and heal me, O Christ.

O GOD, do you rebuke me in your anger?
Do you chasten me in fierce displeasure?
Is it your arrows that pierce me,
your hand come heavy upon me?
With no health in my flesh, do you punish me,
in sternness of love, for my sins?

The tide of my wrongs sweeps over my head,
their weight is a burden too heavy to bear.
My wounds stink and fester through folly,
I am bowed down with grieving all the day long.
My loins are filled with a burning pain,
there is no sound part in my flesh.
I am numbed and stricken to the ground,
I groan in the anguish of my heart.

The pounding of my heart comes to your ears,
my desire for love, my stumbling on the road.
My deep sighing is not hidden from you,
my longing for kindness and the touch that heals.

My heart is in tumult, my strength fails me,
even the light of my eyes has gone from me.
My companions draw back from my affliction,
my kinsfolk stare afar at my sores.

I am like the deaf and hear nothing,
like those whose mouths are sealed.
I have become as one who cannot hear,
in whose mouth there is no retort.

I falter on the edge of the abyss,
my pain is with me continually.
I confess my wickedness with tears,
I shudder with sorrow for my sin.

Refrain:　　From the power of guilt and pain
　　　　　　save me and heal me, O Christ.

Those who seek my life lay their snares,
those who desire my hurt spread evil tales,
murmuring slanders all the day long.
I prayed, Let them never exult over me,
those who laugh harshly when I stumble and fall.

My enemies without cause are strong,
those who hate me wrongfully are many.
Those who repay evil for good are against me,
they blame me for what I did right.

But in you, O God, I have put my trust,
and you will answer me in saving judgment.
Do not forsake me, do not go far from me;
hasten to my help, O God of my salvation.

For I know you enter the heart of our anguish,
you take to yourself the pain of the universe,
you bear the marks of our sins,
you endure and still you forgive.

It is not for our sin that we suffer,
nor for the wrongs of our forebears.
It is that your name may be glorified,
that in us your purpose be known.
Your vulnerable love works without ceasing
to draw us from despair into glory.

Saviour and Healer, present in the midst of our distress, forgiving our sin and relieving our suffering, enable us to deepen our trust in your Spirit at work within us, that your Love may overwhelm us with joy and your Hand guide us in the dance of freedom.

ANGER HUMAN AND DIVINE

Refrain: *Mysterious is the God who throws us to the ground
and continually raises us up.*

I WILL keep watch over my words,
so that I do not offend with my tongue.
I will put a muzzle on my mouth,
while the wicked are in my presence.

How can I keep silent in our day,
as I see the hypocrisies around me,
the poor defrauded of land,
the dwelling place of God dishonoured?

Now that my eyes have been opened,
it is impossible not to be angry.
I cannot be aware and stay calm:
it goes against the grain of my being.

I tried to hold my tongue and say nothing,
refusing to be rash, keeping silent.
But the pain grew intolerable,
my heart burned hot within me.
While I mused the fire burst into flame,
and I spoke from the depth of my being.

Possessed by the demon of anger,
swept along by the vortex of rage,
I was an easy target for the powerful,
a well-aimed blow and I fell.

Yet I need the fire in my belly,
its heat and its light to move me.
I need it to spur me to action,
rage become love in the service of others.

Refrain: *Mysterious is the God who throws us to the ground and continually raises us up.*

Yet I know how fleeting is my life:
O God, let me remember my end,
and the number of my days.
You have made my years but a handsbreath,
my whole span is as nothing before you.

Thinking we stand secure,
we are but a breath of wind,
our lives but a passing shadow.
The riches we heap are like autumn leaves,
golden and brittle to those who gather them.

And now, O God, what is my hope?
Truly my hope is in you.
Deliver me from the trap of my sins,
do not make me the butt of fools.

I was dumb, I did not open my mouth,
silenced now by the thought of my sin.
Your arm is straightening my crookedness,
a pain not easy to bear.

With rebukes you humble me low,
you cause my fair looks to decay,
like a moth you destroy my possessions.
Surely we are but a breath,
as nothing in the sight of your eyes.

Hear my prayer and give ear to my cry:
do not be silent at my tears.
I am but a stranger with you,
a passing guest as my ancestors were.

Turn your anger away from me,
that I may breathe awhile and be glad,
before I go hence
and am no more seen.

So I rely on your kindness alone,
entrusting myself to your mercy,
even to the gates of my death,
down to the depths of the grave.

O God of mysterious anger, may we not imagine you destructive as we are in our rage, but recognize your piercing heat and light serving the truth, your fiercely loving anger overcoming our murdering and mortality, in Jesus Christ our Saviour.

FAITH REJOICING AND FAITH STRUGGLING

Refrain: *In the strivings and rejoicings of faith*
              may our search and our trust give you praise.

I WAITED patiently for you, my God,
and at last you heard my cry.
You lifted me out of the icy torrent,
you drew me out of the quicksand and mire.
You set my feet on solid ground,
making firm my foothold on rock.
No longer am I empty and lost:
you have given my life new meaning.

You have put a new song in my mouth,
a song of thanksgiving and praise.
Many will recognize your wondrous deeds:
they will be glad and put their trust in you.
Blessed are those who have made you their hope,
who have not turned to pride and to lying,
nor to wandering in pursuit of false gods.

Great are the wonderful things you have done,
marvellous are your thoughts and desires.
There is none to be compared with you:
were I to declare everything you have done,
your deeds are more than I am able to express.

We cannot buy your favour with bribes,
you were not pleased with the sacrifices of old.
It is the gift of my heart and my will
that you seek in your long-suffering love.
You have softened the wax in my ears,
I hear you at last and respond:
open and attentive I listen to your voice.

Dear God, I long to do your will.
Your law of love delights my heart.
I have not hidden your salvation in silence,
I have told of your resurrection and glory.
I have not kept back the glad news of deliverance,
your faithfulness, justice, and truth.

So may your truth ever protect me,
your steadfast mercy and love ever be close –
yes, even when troubles overwhelm me,
more numerous than the hairs of my head,
when my sins overtake me and I cannot hear,
and my heart fails within me.

Let those who seek my life to take it away,
let them be put to shame and utterly confounded.
Let those who gloat with the laughter of scorn,
let them be turned back and disgraced.

So may I turn and be glad in you,
so that those who love your salvation may say,
Great and wonderful is God.
In my poverty and need and oppression,
yet you are with me, caring for me.
Yes, I am assured of my faith,
and yes, I still strive to believe.
You are my helper and deliverer:
make no long delay, my Saviour, my God.

O God of truth and mercy, whose voice we miss amidst the distractions and noise
of our lives, penetrate to the core of our being, that we may hear and be glad,
knowing ourselves accepted in your love, able once again to live in your truth and
forgiveness; through Jesus Christ our Saviour.

WHO CONDEMNS?

Refrain: *With judgment and mercy, O God,*
               redeem us in the light of your eyes.

BLESSED are those who care for the poor and the helpless,
who are kind to the outcast within them.
God will deliver them in the day of their trouble,
rescuing the child who is battered and torn.
God will guard them and preserve their life:
they shall be counted as blessed in the land.

O God, you will not give us over to the will of our enemies,
to hatred within and to blame without.
In the day of our calamity you will sustain us,
as warring turbulence threatens our life.

Dear God, be merciful towards me,
heal me for I have sinned against you.
My enemies, within and without, speak evil of me:
"When will you die and your name perish for ever?"

They mouth empty words when they see me,
and mischief stirs in their hearts.
They talk among themselves in the street,
whispering suspicion against me.

They smile at the revealing of my sins,
gloating in triumph at my downfall,
cackling like demons that claw at me,
plucking me down to the mire.

"You are wracked with a deadly disease,
you will not rise again from where you lie."
Even my bosom friend whom I trusted,
who shared my bread, looks down on me.

O God, come down and raise me up,
struggling from the pit in anger and truth,
wrestling with my enemies in my love for them,
dependent together on mercy.
So shall we know that you delight in us,
setting us before your face for ever.

Cleanse my whole being that I may see truly,
that revenge may not brood in my heart.
Keep me from believing all strangers are hostile,
let me see with the eyes of compassion.

May I think good of those who strive against me,
however full of malice seem their hearts.
Heap burning coals of love on our heads:
melt our fears with the flame of your desire.

Burn out from us all that breeds evil,
that we may no longer hurt or destroy.
May we follow the way of justice,
and be redeemed to your glory and joy.

Blessed be God,
the God of all peoples,
at all times and all places,
now and for ever.

Merciful God, prone as we are to blame others and to hate ourselves, take from our eyes the dust that blinds us, that we may treat one another by the light of your compassion, and in the Spirit of Jesus Christ who is the Light of the world.

YEARNING FOR GOD

Refrain: *Why are you so full of heaviness, O my soul,*
              and why so rebellious within me?
              Put your trust in God,
              patiently wait for the dawn,
              and you will then praise
              your deliverer and your God.

As a deer longs for streams of water,
so longs my soul for you, O God.
My soul is thirsty for the living God:
when shall I draw near to see your face?
My tears have been my food in the night:
all day long they ask me, Where now is your God?
As I pour out my soul in distress,
I remember how I went to the temple of God,
with shouts and songs of thanksgiving,
a multitude keeping high festival.

My soul is heavy within me: therefore I remember you
from the land of Jordan and from the hills of Hermon.
Deep calls to deep in the roar of the waterfalls,
all your waves and your torrents have gone over me.
Surely, O God, you will show me mercy in the daytime,
and at night I will sing your praise, O God my God.
I will say to God, my rock, Why have you forgotten me?
Why must I go like a mourner because the enemy oppresses me?
Like a sword piercing my bones, my enemies have mocked me,
asking me all day long, Where now is your God?

O God, take up my cause and strive for me
with a godless people that knows no mercy.
Save me from the grip of cunning and lies,
for you are my God and my strength.
Why must you cast me away from your presence?
Why must I be clothed in rags, humiliated by my enemy?
✔ O send out your light and your truth and let them lead me,
let them guide me to your holy hill and to your dwelling.
Then I shall go to the altar of God, the God of my joy and
    delight,
and to the harp I shall sing your praises, O God my God.

*Loving God, as we join our cries with those who are deeply depressed and in
despair, renew in us the spirit of hope, the yearning for life in you alone, and the
expectancy that even when every door is closed, yet you will surprise us with joy.*

CAST OFF BY GOD?

Refrain: *Is the wood of the cross now in splinters?*
            Does the tree of salvation still stand?

WE have heard with our ears, O God,
our ancestors have told us,
what things you did in their days,
how you drove out the tribes before us
and caused us to root and to grow.
For it was not by their swords
that they possessed the land,
nor did their own power get them the victory,
but your right hand, your holy arm,
and the light of your countenance upon them.
It was out of sheer love that you did this,
out of your care and delight.

You reign over us their descendants:
by your power do we strike our enemies:
in your name alone do we tread them down.
We do not trust in long bow and sword,
but only in you to deliver us,
putting our adversaries to confusion.
In you alone is our boast,
giving thanks to your name without ceasing.

But now you have cast us off and brought us to shame,
you do not go out with our armies.
You have given us as sheep to be butchered,
and our foes plunder us at will.
You have scattered us among the nations,
and made a profitless sale.
You have made us the scorn of our neighbours,
mocked and derided by those around us.

You have made us a byword among the peoples:
they dismiss us with eyes full of hatred.
Our disgrace is before us all the day long,
and shame has covered our face,
at the voice of the slanderer and reviler,
at the sight of the enemy and avenger.

All this calamity has fallen upon us,
even though we have not forgotten you.
We have not betrayed your covenant,
our hearts have not turned back,
nor have our steps strayed from your paths.

Yet you have crushed us in the haunts of jackals,
and covered us with the deepest darkness.
If we had forgotten your name,
or stretched out our hands to strange gods,
would you not have searched it out,
knowing as you do the secrets of our hearts?
But for your sake we are killed all the day long,
we are counted as sheep for the slaughter.

Rouse yourself, O God, why do you sleep?
Awake, do not cast us off for ever.
Why do you hide your face
and forget our misery and oppression?
Our souls are bowed to the dust,
our bellies cleave to the ground.
Arise, O God, and help us,
and redeem us for your mercy's sake.

Strange how all this should surprise us –
the evil we thought was elsewhere
runs through the heart of each one of us.
No wonder we sense your eclipse, O God,
boasting you are always behind us.

Refrain: *Is the wood of the cross now in splinters?*
               Does the tree of salvation still stand?

Renew in us your covenant with Earth,
that we may respect one another,
even those who hate and despise us.
However oppressed we may be,
and must strive to disarm the oppressor,
keep hope of your forgiveness alive,
transform our thirst for revenge,
bring us home with weeping and joy.

And yet we are being too kind,
too easy and bland in the face of great evil?
What of the cry of the Holocaust,
of the sheep slaughtered by jackals?
What of the voice of those without name,
a number, a badge, for aliens despised?
Naked they went to the chambers of gas,
hair, clothes and rings left behind.
Their corpses were piled into ovens,
their ashes scattered on lakes that were bitter.

What of those who drove the trains,
who herded like cattle folk like ourselves,
who patrolled the barbed wire of the camps,
who delivered by lorry the canisters of gas?
What of those who locked the doors,
who put out the lights, melted the gold,
who turned their skin into lampshades?

O God, why are you silent?
O God, answer those who accuse you.
Why have you forgotten the wretched of the earth?
What profit do you gain from this their affliction?

*O God of Love – if indeed you are Love, for the howls of suffering have hidden
your face – show us again in the Crucified One the eyes telling us that you are
there, at the heart of the desolate cries.*

A ROYAL CELEBRATION

Refrain: *Clothe us with the splendour and glory*
that shines through justice and mercy.

My heart is aflame with fine phrases,
I make my song for the great king:
my tongue is the pen of a skilled writer.
You are the fairest of the children of earth:
grace flows from your lips,
for God has blessed you for ever and ever.

Take the sword to protect the weak,
defeating those who would threaten them.
Ride on in the cause of truth,
and for the sake of justice and mercy.
Your enemies will do well to tremble,
your arrows will be sharp in their hearts.

Your divine throne endures for ever,
the sceptre of your realm is a sceptre of equity.
You love righteousness and hate evil:
so God has anointed you with the oil of gladness,
choosing you to serve for the sake of the people.

Your garments are fragrant with myrrh, aloes, and cassia:
music from ivory palaces makes your heart glad.
Daughters of kings are among your noble women:
the queen is at your side in gold of Ophir.

Hear, O daughter, consider and incline your ear:
forget your own people and your father's house.
The king desires your beauty:
he is your lord: bow down before him.
The richest among the people, O daughter of Tyre,
shall entreat your favour with gifts.

Refrain: *Clothe us with the splendour and glory
that shines through justice and mercy.*

The princess in her chamber is being robed
with garments of cloth of gold.
In robes of brilliant colours
she is led to your presence, O king.
Her bridesmaids follow in procession,
with joy and gladness they form her train:
they enter the palace with songs of delight.

So the generations pass,
as children grow strong and their elders fade.
May the old become wise and the young bring us hope.
And I will make God's name known,
whose reign has no end.
All the peoples will praise you, O God,
throughout the generations.

We praise you, O God,
for the gift of yourself in the Infant King:
Jesus, sovereign ruler of all,
in whom is our royal destiny too:
celebrants at the banquet of heaven,
guests at the great marriage feast,
gloriously singing in triumphal procession,
our ancestors and descendants with us,
joyful in the communion of saints.

Dear God, we offer you our lives this day,
the gift of love in our hearts and our loins,
the incense of prayer, the myrrh of our suffering,
the gold of all that we hold most dear,
that you may create through our loyal obedience,
such wonders as pass our imagining.

*Lift up our hearts, O glorious God, and renew in us the hope of a marvellous
destiny, a life of incomparable splendour, crowned with the love and peace that
pass understanding, in Jesus Christ, our Servant-King.*

THE GOD OF POWERS

Refrain: *You are for us the God of the powers,*
                   a safe stronghold, the God of all peoples.

GOD is our refuge and strength,
a very present help in time of trouble.
Therefore we shall not be afraid,
even though the earth be moved,
even though the mountains should crumble
and fall into the sea,
even though the waters should foam and rage,
assault the cliffs and make them shudder.

There is a river whose streams make glad the city of God.
Here is God's dwelling place and it will stand firm.
God's rescue dawns like the morning light,
God's voice echoes through every land.
When powerful nations panic and totter
and the whole world comes crashing down,

Come and see, stand in awe
at the powerful things God will do on the earth,
putting an end to all war in the world,
breaking the bow, shattering the spear into splinters,
throwing our weapons on the fire.
"Be still and know that I am God:
exalted among the nations,
my name known at last on the earth."

*At the still centre of the turning world, may we simply rest and be, trusting again
the promise that all shall be made new in the bringing of the powers of this world
to serve the purposes of God's greater Peace.*

THE WORSHIP OF THE PEOPLE OF GOD

Refrain: *As citizens of one world*
            your people give you praise.

CLAP your hands, all you peoples:
cry aloud to God with shouts of joy.
Approach the presence of God with awe,
the great sovereign over all the earth.

O God, you have called us to serve the peoples,
that they may come to acknowledge your glory.
You have made us stewards of your gifts,
that we may not boast and be proud.
You have loved us and blessed us with a goodly heritage,
overflowing with all that we need.

Let us join the procession in praise of your name,
with trumpets and horns and the sound of rejoicing.
We sing praises, sing praises to you, O God,
we sing praises, sing praises to your name.

For you are sovereign over all the earth:
let us praise your name with well-wrought psalm.
You are the ruler of all the peoples,
wise and just in your dealings.

Those who give counsel gather together
as the people of the God of Abraham.
For even the mighty ones of the earth
are become the servants of God,
the God who is greatly to be praised.

Living, loving God, draw the peoples of faith closer together, ancient and ever-new, that we may worship you today in spirit and in truth.

THE CITY OF GOD

Refrain: *May the cities and lands of this world*
be transformed by the Spirit of God.

O GOD, you are greatly to be praised
in the city of your dwelling place.
High and beautiful is the holy mountain:
it is the joy of the whole earth.

Here on Mount Zion stands the city
where you reign with just and steady hand.
Your rule is firm and secure,
strong as the walls and ramparts.

Strangers who approach are amazed,
the powerful of the earth dumbfounded.
Trembling takes hold of the proud,
anguish seizes the hostile,
like the howl of the harsh east wind
that splinters the ships on the rocks.

We call your mercies to mind,
here in the midst of your temple.
You govern the peoples with justice,
even to the ends of the earth.

Pilgrim, walk round the city,
count all her towers,
examine her walls with care,
consider well her strongholds.

So may we tell those who come after,
that here they may rest secure,
for our God reigns for ever and ever,
who will guide us to all eternity.

Refrain: *May the cities and lands of this world*
              be transformed by the Spirit of God.

Such was the place of your worship and dwelling,
sacred, O God, to your people of old.
Now may you dwell in each of our hearts,
may every city be the place of your dwelling.

So may we worship you in spirit and truth,
may recognize you in streets and in squares,
in a common life of justice and peace,
in compassion and freedom under the law.

Bring the light, O God, that will one day shine
brighter than the sun and the moon and the stars,
the light of the Christ to illumine the dark,
the face that transfigures the city to glory.

*Gracious God, you have called us to the freedom of your City. So shape our lives
in the ways of justice that we may become worthy of that citizenship that you have
bestowed upon us, in the communion of your saints and in the fellowship of Jesus
Christ.*

THE HOLLOWNESS OF WEALTH

Refrain: *Where your treasure is,*
             there will your heart be also.

HEAR this, all you peoples;
listen, inhabitants of the world,
all children of the earth,
both rich and poor together.
My mouth shall speak wisdom,
the thoughts of my heart be full of understanding.
I will reveal the secret of a riddle,
unfolding a mystery to the sound of the lyre.

Why should I be afraid in times of trouble,
when the cruel and the greedy triumph,
those who put their trust in great wealth,
and boast of the abundance of their riches?

No one may ransom a sister or brother,
no one give God a price for them,
so that they may live for ever
and never see the grave:
to ransom their lives is so costly
we must abandon the idea for ever.

For we see the prosperous die,
and perish with the foolish and ignorant,
leaving their wealth to others.
The tomb is their home for ever,
their dwelling through all generations,
despite their estates named after them.
The wealthy in all their pomp –
they are just like the beasts – they perish.

Refrain: *Where your treasure is,*
          there will your heart be also.

This is the lot of the arrogant,
who are pleased with their words
and trust in themselves.
They are destined to die like sheep:
death is their shepherd,
they cannot avoid their end.
Their good looks will fade in the tomb,
and their grandeur will follow them.

But God will ransom my life,
God will snatch me from the power of the grave.
I will not be afraid when neighbours grow rich,
when the wealth of their households increases.
For they will take nothing away when they die,
nor will their wealth go down to them.

Though they thought highly of themselves while they lived,
and were praised for their worldly success,
they will go to the company of their ancestors,
who will never again see the sun.
The wealthy in all their pomp –
they are just like the beasts – they perish.

Living God, may our contemplation of death free us from envy and greed, that we may be content to travel light in this world, undistracted by the babel of possessions and in the Spirit of the One who had nowhere to lay his head, Jesus Christ our Saviour.

THE JUDGMENT OF GOD

Refrain: *Your eyes are fierce with love,*
  your hands are gentle in judgment.

FROM the midst of the glory of the sun,
from the mountain top of your appearing,
you come to us in perfect beauty,
the judge of the earth doing all things well.

You come to us, you do not keep silent,
you sear us with the flames of your truth,
you devour the chaff of our sins:
awesome is this face of your love.

We have failed to worship you in truth,
we have been disloyal to your covenant,
content with repeating mere words,
self-important in the display of our ceremonies.

We have not obeyed your will,
colluding with those who thieve and betray,
loosening our tongues in slander and gossip,
even lying against kith and kin.

Open our eyes and ears, O God,
we who have been so blind and deaf,
seduced by the glamour and dazzle around us,
lulled by the weavers of magic with words.

No better are we than your people of old,
seeking to please you with smoking burnt sacrifice,
thinking you relished animals' flesh,
that this was the worship you sought.

But all the beasts of the forest are yours,
and so are the cattle on a thousand hills;
you know all the birds of the air,
the grasshoppers of the field are in your sight.

Refrain: *Your eyes are fierce with love,*
              your hands are gentle in judgment.

You own the very gifts that we bring you,
all things come to us from out of your hand.
You give them to us to enjoy
and to share with others in need.

Sacrificial love is the altar of worship
where you touch the lives of the needy,
humbled as we are by all that you give us,
judged by those more generous than we.

Renew in us the covenant of old,
may we be faithful to the promises we made,
the vows over gifts to be holy with you,
in deed and in truth to follow your way.

You thunder so fiercely in love for us,
you whisper so gently in judgment,
lowering the walls of defence
that surround our self-centred complaints.

So often we live for ourselves,
indifferent to the needs of the oppressed,
passing by the homeless under the arches,
refusing to hear how you judge us through them.

Turn us around, compassionate judge,
show us the face of your pain:
it is we who add to your burden,
as you endure the cost of redeeming.

In the day of our need we cry out to you,
offering our sorrowing hearts,
trusting that you will forgive us,
and refine us in the flame of your love.

*Come, living Christ, with burning coals and purge our lips; come with the
judgment that saves and gives us back our sense of worth because it matters what
we do; come with passionate desire and sweep us into your arms; come with the
love that will not let us go.*

PSALMS 51–100

THE UTTER MERCY OF GOD

Refrain: Create in me a clean heart, O God,
and renew a right spirit within me.

Enfold me in your love, dear God,
yet/pierce my heart with your mercy.
In the cascading of your compassion
scour away all that offends.
Wash me thoroughly from my wickedness,
and cleanse me from my sin.

My/failures weigh heavy on my heart,
my sin confronts me at the turning of the road.
Against you alone have I sinned, my Beloved,
doing what is evil and causing more harm.
In the eyes of my victims your judgment is clear:
there is nothing I can claim in your presence.

I was/formed in the midst of a world gone wrong,
from the moment of my conceiving I breathed my ancestors' sin.
The truths to which I am blind are hidden so deep, so secretly:
bring the light of your wisdom to the depths of my heart.

Bathe me in water that is fresh from the spring,
wash me/and I shall be whiter than snow.
Make me hear of joy and gladness,
that the bones which you have broken may dance again.
Turn your face from my twists and deceits,
blot out all my misdeeds.

Cast me not away from your presence,
and take not your Holy Spirit from me.
Give me the comfort of your help again,
and strengthen me with your courage and hope.

Refrain: Create in me a clean heart, O God,
and renew a right spirit within me.

Then I shall teach your ways to those around me,
and others will be converted to your path.
Deliver us all from guilt of bloodshed, O God,
for you are the God of the world that is coming.
In health and truth we shall sing of your justice.
When you open my lips, O God,
my mouth shall sing of your praise.

For you desire no animal sacrifices,
no formal gifts out of mere duty.
You do not delight in burnt offerings,
nothing from our wealth can buy your favour.
The sacrifice you ask is a troubled spirit;
it is my pride that must yield.
My broken and contrite heart I bring,
so foolish, self-centred, and vain;
and yet it is all that I have.
Even this gift you will not despise,
for I hear again that you yearn for me,
with a love I can barely imagine.

So do I give you the whole of myself,
dependent as I am on the gift of your mercy.
So may my giving to others
be free of the motives of power,
gifts that overwhelm or appease.
May my heart be spontaneously giving,
spreading delight and mutual embrace.
Such is the way of the City of Peace,
whose walls you call us to build.

Take us to yourself, Compassionate God, we who hurt so much in the
depths of our being, caught up in the pain of life, and so often inflicting yet
more on to others; embrace us with the hands that show still the mark of
nails, your love swallowing up all our sin and pride. So we pray that broken
bones may joy, in the dance of Jesus our Redeemer.

THE LIE AND THE TRUTH

Refrain: Keep our eyes fixed on the truth,
the truth that will set us free.

So often the powerful ones of the world
seem to boast of their mischief and pride.
They trust in the abundance of wealth,
they take perverse delight in their greed.

They contrive destroying slanders:
their tongues cut sharp like a razor.
In love with evil they refuse the good:
telling lies, the truth is far from them.
They love words that harm and devour,
and every deceit of the tongue.

They step on one another as they climb to power,
they thrust the weak to the gutter;
seducing the gullible in the magic of words,
they trample the truth in pursuit of ambition.

O God, break them down utterly,
uproot them from the land of the living,
topple them from their Babel of lies,
throw them down to the dust.

Yet so often we are the powerful,
if only with family and friends.
We wound with whispers of gossip,
mockery and scorn in our hearts,
bitterness souring our lips.

Refrain: Keep our eyes fixed on the truth,
the truth that will set us free.

We have not trusted your goodness, O God,
our hearts have not been grateful.
We have not glorified your name,
neither by word nor by deed.

Too easy to call on God to destroy,
hard to be humbled by words that are true.
Even as we cry for the righting of wrongs,
for the destruction of those who harm others,
those who crush the weak and defenceless,
so do we know that revenge solves nothing,
annihilation reaping more violence still.

May your Spirit go deeper within us,
purging our hearts, burning the impure.
Hold at bay our murderous words.
May we strive with the angel of justice,
living the way of your truth and your Word,
our faces etched in the fierceness of Love.

Keep before us the vision of a life that is whole:
may we no longer grasp at material things.
Like a green tree may we spread out our branches,
to shield the passerby from the heat,
offering the traveller refreshment and rest,
in quietness and confidence living for others,
people of truth and compassion,
oases of God in the most barren of lands.

May our eyes turn to look again on you, O Christ. For you are the Way, the
Truth, and the Life. Give us courage always to be loyal to the Truth, to
follow wherever the Way may lead, costly though it be, trusting that the goal
is none other than Life in you.

FLESH OF OUR FLESH

God walks the earth,
a wandering Jew,
a holy fool,
in search of justice.

Acid in the rain shrivels the leaves,
the wind rattles in the city's throat,
Cancerous fish float down the rivers,
even the innocent grass is corrupted.

We have become as appetites in nightmares,
as horses of apocalypse with thundering hooves,
like monsters with ravening jaws,
devouring what was given us to cherish.

God walks the earth,
a poor man in rags,
peering into the darkness
for one face of trust.

We have raped the good earth and her peoples,
tearing them apart to satisfy greed.
We have relished the flesh of our neighbours,
like lions tearing their prey.

The powerful prepare a cannibal feast,
harsh eyes glint in the sharpening knives.
They have become as flesh-eating gods;
we, blind consumers, we follow them.

God walks towards us,
vulnerable as flesh,
a body broken,
blood shed.

Weighed down with bloodlust our footing slips,
we begin to drown in the floods of despair.
O God, grasp the hand stretched out in panic,
before we vanish for ever and are no more seen.

Forgetting the early days of our pain,
afraid of the intimacy we desperately crave,
we have speared the flesh of our neighbour,
refusing to draw near in healing embrace.

*Intimate God, Flesh of our flesh, Earth of our earth, reveal to us the anger
and malice, the greed and pride, that mask our pain; enable us to withdraw
the spear of our revenge from the flesh of others and from your flesh, O God.
Enclose our hurt in your side that we have wounded, and draw us closer to
one another in compassion and forgiveness, dependent utterly on your mercy
and acceptance.*

A CRY OF COMPLAINT

Refrain: O God, act soon.

Helpless, hemmed in, we are trapped by the powerful;
the insolent lash out with their tongue.
The ruthless sweep away what we thought were our homes,
the ignorant blame us because we are poor.

O God, are you not more powerful than they?
Why do you not speed them down to their doom?
Sweep them away who would treat us as worthless,
that we may feast our eyes on their fall.

What kind of God are you, my helper?
Why do you not show the strength of your arm?
You have promised to put an end to their power,
yet the promise remains unfulfilled.

Just once we have seen the world overturned,
your Chosen One vulnerable yet strong,
absorbing the evil thrown by the powerful,
triumphant through death in the ways of your love.

To keep trust with you taxes our faith,
to praise you in our days with hearts that are glad.
Why do you let the powerful still trample us down,
how can we believe when a child screams with pain?

Yet still we desire the face of your love,
to praise you in wonder for all that you do,
to know the scales fall from our eyes,
to dance the way of freedom hand in hand with the powerful.

Spirit of the living God, deftly and quickly probe the diseased heart of our
world, and dissolve the evil encrusted there, that healed of our wounds and
rescued from our wrong, we may no longer oppress but set one another free,
in that same Spirit of Jesus Christ our Saviour.

DAYS OF BETRAYAL IN THE CITY

Refrain: Renew the covenant of your love, O God:
may we in truth be your friends.

In these our days of turmoil,
of restlessness and complaint,
we accuse and betray one another,
lashing out in the fury of pain.

We set on one another with greed,
we persecute with baying and clamour.
We see slaughter and our hearts writhe,
the horrors of dying overwhelm us.

Violence reigns in the streets of the city,
vicious dogs snarl at the stranger.
Fraud flits through the market place,
greed wins softly behind baize doors.

My eyes flash wild with horror,
my limbs quake and I cannot still them.
My heart grows cold through fear,
the ice of death grips me.

I said. O for the wings of a dove,
that I might fly away and be at rest.
I yearn to flee to the mountains,
to make my dwelling in the wilderness.

O for a refuge of peace,
out of the blast of slander,
far from the tempest of calumny,
from the harsh wind of the double-tongued.

For it was not an enemy who taunted me,
or I might have been able to bear it.
It was not a foe who was so insolent,
or I might have hidden myself away.

But it was you, my equal,
my companion, my familiar friend.
Ours was a pleasant harmony
as we walked side by side to the house of our God.

You have not kept your word,
you have no love of God in your heart,
and have broken the covenant you have sworn,
deserting those who were at peace with you.

Your mouth is smooth as butter,
yet war is in your heart.
Your words are softer than oil,
yet your sword flashes in the dark.

My heart cries out in anguish and grief,
Get out of my sight, you hypocrite!
Go down in terror to your grave, you betrayer,
for you have worked treachery among us.

Yet how I yearn for the healing of pain,
for a love grown cold to kindle again.
I pray to you, God, that we may be reconciled,
drawn again to the way of your justice.

Humble the pride in us all,
your love and your power consistent forever.
May we lift the weight of oppression,
may our enemies release the spring of their traps.

I cast my burden on you, O God,
and you will sustain and encourage me.
I will call from the midst of my groaning,
you will redeem me to healing and peace.

My heart has been so constricted,
my affections so easily hurt.
Yet your arms are wide and welcoming,
in your presence we are relaxed,
and feel most strangely at home.

O living God, whose love has been betrayed and denied over and over again, whose covenants have been torn apart, forgive our lack of trust and loyalty, and call us to yourself again, we who bear the marks of Judas and of Cain.

EMPTY AND AFRAID, YET TRUSTING

Refrain: I will put my trust in you, O God,
I will praise you for your Presence.
I will trust and not be afraid:
what can mortal flesh do to me?

The echo of the infant sounds,
the unwanted child cries for affection.
The giver of my life is my adversary,
persistently pressing upon me.
I feel nothing but hatred towards me,
I stand on no ground of my worth.
Are my tears counted in your flask,
are my hurts noted in your book?

I feel I am dying before I am born,
my feet slip from under me.
Empty and distressed, I am nothing,
yet I yearn for life to the full.

From the midst of my wasteland
of needs never met,
knowing my emptiness,
I wait to be filled.

Rain on the desert of my terror,
fill my empty soul to overflowing,
that I may joy in the life that you give,
a river that will flow to those who are parched.

As Mary opened her will, her heart, and her womb, giving her emptiness to be filled with your living presence, so, Giver of life, encourage us to be empty and open before you, that, being born in us, you may displace all our fear and distress.

IDENTITY IN THE CITY

*Refrain: Be exalted, O God, in your little ones,
let your glory shine in our streets.*

The crowds on the pavements jostle me,
the drone of the traffic wearies me.
In the shadow of your wings I find refuge,
beneath your hovering presence I find peace.

The faces of strangers stare through me;
aimless I wander, there is nowhere I belong.
In the compassion of your face I find mercy,
in you and you alone do I know who I am.

I fear the hard glint in their eyes,
whose teeth snap from behind locked doors.
In the faithfulness of your promise I trust,
giving us freedom and wide open space.

Their faces look careworn and hollow,
grey like the evening and houses around.
Let melody break through the gloom,
the trumpet and flute to awaken the morning.

Compassion and care is locked in each one of us,
faithful and kind we all long to be.
Melt the fear in our hearts of the stranger we meet,
that we may open our arms in vulnerable embrace.

*O God of freedom, unlock the hearts of your people who strive to be human
in the city, that your love may cast out fear, and that we may know again
that we belong to one another and to you.*

WHAT KIND OF VENGEANCE?

Refrain: The faces of the downtrodden accuse us:
only the poor can redeem.

Do you decree what is just, O rulers of the nations?
With justice do you judge the peoples of the earth?
No, you work in the land with an evil heart,
you relish the violence you have wrought.
The wicked are estranged even from the womb,
they are liars that go astray from the day of their birth.

They are poisonous with the venom of serpents,
like the deaf asp that stops its ears,
that will not heed the voice of the charmers,
though the binder of spells be skilful.

Break their teeth, O God, in their mouths,
shatter the jaws of the young lions, O God.
Let them vanish like water that drains away,
let them be trodden down and wither like grass,
like a woman's miscarriage that passes away,
like an abortive birth that sees not the sun.

Let them be cut down like thorns before they know it,
like brambles swept angrily aside.
The just shall rejoice when they see your vengeance,
they will wash their feet in the blood of the wicked.
People will say, There is a reward for the virtuous,
for the wicked there comes the judgment of God...

Purge away from me, O God,
all malice and hatred, all bitterness of memory.
Stop my rejoicing at the pain of their doom,
even the worst of those who oppressed me.

Refrain: The faces of the downtrodden accuse us:
only the poor can redeem.

Only so can I hope to stand in your presence,
for you read all my ways and my heart,
all its murky unease and its fickleness.
We are all unjust, disordered, and lawless,
hardly sensing the lure of your love:
we can but know it as wrath.

Withhold your Light – it will blind us,
yet let us not perish in the dark and the cold.
Gradually warm the hearts that are frozen,
till the depths of the darkness dazzle.

Have mercy upon us, have mercy,
criminals and judges with the roughest of justice.
No plea can we enter before you.
It is the deprived and homeless, ragged and shivering,
who stand in the dock to accuse us.

Those on the edge, unkempt, unacceptable,
they are the ones who show us your face.
And, deep within, is a child who is shunned,
whom we treat as our enemy, battered and bruised.

O when will we learn to stretch out our arms,
to receive from the outcasts and scapegoats
the redeeming embrace and the melting of tears:
in them and them only is our last dying hope.

Harness the seething power of our anger, O God, the whirlpools of rage, the
waves of indignation, and channel this awesome energy in the ways of your
justice and love, in Jesus Christ our Doom and our Saviour.

FOR THE IMPRISONED AND TORTURED

*Refrain: Judge and saviour of the world,
have mercy upon us, have mercy.*

Cruel men roam the streets in the darkness,
howling like dogs, they prowl round the city,
They snarl and snap as they seize their prey,
they growl if their desire is frustrated.

I pray for the tortured and victims of malice,
for those imprisoned for no fault of their own.
My feelings run high – God forgive my excess –
why is your mercy and justice delayed?

Deliver the oppressed from the terrors of evil,
free them from those who relish their pain.
For the savage stir up violence against them,
waiting to knock at the door before dawn.

They keep the peacemakers distracted and tense,
breaking their spirit, mauling their flesh,
and all for no sin or transgression,
or any crime for which they are guilty.

The oppressed look to you, God their strength:
arise from your sleep and do not delay.
May your eyes flash with judgment and truth,
silencing the treacherous and false.

Show them the height of their pride,
reveal to them the lie they have lived.
Bind them so that their power is removed,
bring to their eyes the tears of repentance.

In your great love run to meet those who suffer,
show them the ruin of those who oppressed them.
Yet slay not the wicked, copying their ways,
but make them powerless to harm, and bring them to truth.

Refrain: Judge and Saviour of the world,
have mercy upon us, have mercy.

O God, from the depth of your love bearing pain,
break the cycle of our wraths and our sorrows.
For you are not a God who destroys,
you seek always to redeem and renew.

And so I will sing of your love and your power,
I will sing in the morning and tell of your goodness.
For you have been our strong tower,
a sure refuge in the day of distress.
I will sing your praise, O God my strength,
for you are my kraal for ever.

O God, seeking always to create at the heart of our evil and pain, sustaining
life in all your creatures and present with them in their distress, let us not
fall beyond your reach, and raise us by forgiveness and healing to a new love
for one another and for you.

THE WAR OF THE UNHOLY

Refrain: Turn us O God from our slaughter,
yet keep us striving for truth.

Echoes of warriors sound through the years,
we are zealous for God, holy our war.
We shout for you, our God, resplendent in armour,
your banner unfurled as we sweep into battle.

The fleet sails and our eyes shine;
our cause is just, our God is with us.
You are angry, O God, with our enemies –
we can slaughter them all, feeling no shame.

O God, do not be lukewarm and bland:
be provoked still by our enemies.
Do not storm out of sight through the dust,
leaving us to tremble in fear.

Yet you vanished from our sight: where were you?
You betrayed your promise to be with us.
Wounded and weary, we limp back defeated;
bewildered, we cling to your flag.

Are we far from the cry of the zealot,
from the mob who follow the drumbeat?
So easy to spit out the slogans of hate,
to become like those who oppose us.

So easy to swoop on the spoil,
to claim another parcel of land,
to grind the poor to submission,
to be drunk on the shedding of blood.

Refrain: Turn us O God from our slaughter,
yet keep us striving for truth.

Though we cling to belief in your blessing,
you are the God of island and continent,
and we but one race spread over the earth,
not one of us favoured above all the rest.

Our common greed and our fear of each other,
our desire for Mammon grown to excess,
our zeal for being right and others so wrong,
these are our enemies now.

In your name alone will we triumph,
content to be stewards of earth,
to live in justice with our neighbours,
the power of the fanatic taken away.

Forgive us, O God, for stubbornly continuing to picture you with iron fist,
for claiming that you are always on our side. Renew the vision of you as wise
and just guardian of the people, curbing the power of those who would
harm, bearing in yourself what is yet unresolved. Keep us steady and true,
that those we now perceive as our enemies may come to be our partners in the
work of your creating.

HOPE IN GOD ALONE

Refrain: In our despair give us hope;
in our death give us life.

I stand on a rock at the edge of the sea,
the wind hurls the spray at my face.
The depths of the ocean swell heavy with menace,
tides of despair drown my heart in the deep.

I collapse by a rock in the wastes of the desert,
the noonday sun scorches my skin.
Waves of heat beat upon my weary heart,
my eyes stare at the dry bones around me.

The spirit has gone out of me,
my self-centred desires are as nothing.
I have come to the brink of inner death,
I descend to the depths of my doom.

Rescue me, O God, pity the pitiful,
lend me the strength of your tower of rock.
Succour me under your hovering wings,
welcome me into your hospitable home.

My vows lie broken, yet would I serve you,
my heart's desire is to love your name.
May the angels of mercy and truth stand by me,
the hand of deliverance heal me.

With a glimmer of hope I remember your love,
the love that finds me even as I search.
You have entered the void of my despair,
meeting me in the very place of your absence.

The music of praise sounds again in my heart,
the words of rejoicing take shape on my lips.
You renew my strength to fulfil what I promise,
the name that you give me endures through the years.

Implacable God, face us with the truth that we have no power of ourselves to help ourselves. Raise us from the depths of exhaustion and despair, and renew in us the spirit of life and hope, in Jesus Christ our Redeemer.

HOLDING STEADILY TO GOD

Refrain: Keep our eyes fixed on the goal,
Christ in us, the hope of our glory.

In the depths of my being I become quiet and still:
I wait for you, my God, source of my salvation.
You are a sure and steady rock, watching over me,
so that I shall not fall to my doom.

I am afraid of the powerful who overwhelm me,
cowards who encircle me, towering above me.
They are like a battering ram to a crumbling wall,
they exult in their lust for destruction.

Their delight is only in lies;
the truth is far from their hearts.
They utter words that are softer than butter;
inwardly they do but curse.

Nevertheless, I hold steadily to you:
you are my hope, my rock, my salvation.
In the stillness I wait for your presence:
you watch over me, I shall not fall to my doom. /

In you, O God, is my health and glory,
the rock of my faith; in you is my trust.
I pour out my whole being in your presence:
in you I place all my hope. /

In very truth we are but a breath of wind:
faithless and fearful, we have betrayed you.
Put us in the balance and we can only rise:
we are lighter than a feather in the wind.

Let us not trust in extortion and robbery,
let us not put on the masks of vanity.
When riches and possessions increase,
let us not set our heart upon them.

Refrain: Keep our eyes fixed on the goal,
            Christ in us, the hope of our glory.

For then we should become like the powerful,
betraying you again with our love of money,
trampling the face of the poor in the mire,
holding on to wealth by means of the lie.

Teach me again, O God, the truth of your name:
to you alone belongs power,
in you alone do we find mercy.
What reward could there be for our work?

*May the powerful of the land know their own failings and fears, and their
need for forgiveness, that they may empower the oppressed, temper the law
with mercy, and work for the common good, always holding before them the
vision of the Commonwealth of God.*

THE CITY-DWELLER'S DESERT

Refrain: Sustain me through the dry places,
bring me to the beautiful country.

In the depths of my being you are my God,
at the rising of the sun I seek your face.
My heart thirsts for you, my flesh longs for you,
in a barren and dry land where no water is.

I search for you in unexpected places,
at the edges of the known, in the language of dreams,
in the wilderness of the city streets,
in the grim towers where the desperate dwell.

There may I look long and lovingly,
there may I listen for the word beyond words,
there may I wait for a glimpse of your glory,
there may I utter strange songs of your praise.

For your love endures to the end,
it is better even than life itself.
So shall my lips praise you,
and I shall lift up my hands in your name.

With food, shelter, and clothing we shall be content;
with simple dignity we shall be rich in friends.
The streets and squares of the city will be our meeting place,
among the trees of the parks we shall breathe free and play.

With manna in my exile do you feed me,
with water springing up from parched land.
I am deeply satisfied with a sumptuous feast,
my whole being resounds with murmurs of joy.

Refrain: Sustain me through the dry places,
bring me to the beautiful country.

Courage have I found to face the creatures of the night,
the terrible faces masking cries of abandonment,
swords that glint in the darkness protecting the weak,
jackals that swoop on those who dare near.

I am bewildered by mirrors distorting the truth,
lost before hallucinations spun in the heat.
Yet will I trust you through the blindness of light,
through the delusions that threaten to destroy me.

I hear your voice, Do not be afraid.
You sustain me in the watches of the night,
your hovering wings give me shade on my journey.
I stumble, yet I trust you not to let go.

The faces of terror will prove my friends yet,
guarding as they do my fragile soul-self,
waiting the calm word of the approach of true love,
waiting to be named as faithful and true.

So shall I emerge to the place of rejoicing,
the child and the adult linked arm in arm.
We shall see your face in all your creatures,
we shall know the truth in our hearts.

Pioneer of the living way, give us courage to traverse the waste and barren
places, trusting that we shall come at the last to our true home and to the city
of our God.

BEWILDERED BY CRUELTY

Refrain: I reel from blows of the enemy:
where can my heart find ease?

Hear me, O God, from the depths of my being,
fearful as I am of being destroyed.
Who are these enemies that swirl around me,
who conspire against me in a hostile world?

How have I released this torrent of abuse?
Whence come these arrows of bitter words?
Those whom I thought were my friends
pile all my faults on my tired spirit.

No innocence, O God, would I pretend,
my failure and guilt are too real.
But it feels they were planning in secret,
ready to pounce from a place unseen.

Through the years they smiled and spoke tenderly:
now the lash of their tongues is unleashed.
They have laid their mines with such skill –
they have even forgotten they did so –
and they blame me for stepping upon them.

Perhaps they did not even know what they did,
so dark and deep is the human heart.
They dare not face the truth of their pain:
they seek revenge for hurts unremembered.

Deliver me, O God, from the paralysis of fear,
from the confusions of my mind and the turmoil of my heart.
I am consumed with anxiety and dread,
the hovering unknown fills me with terror.

Refrain: I reel from the blows of the enemy:
where can my heart find ease?.

The sky seems full of probing eyes,
an unseen lens orbits the earth.
Ears hide in dim corners of the room,
the wavelengths carry our secret thoughts.

Reveal them to themselves, O God,
bring them down for the evil they have spoken,
those who say they hate only my sin,
but who slay me in the name of your justice.

Let the devices of our hearts be made known,
your arrows of truth piercing our confusions.
Reveal us in scorching light to one another,
that we may lay down our weapons and forgive.

Even now we rejoice and give thanks to your name,
the distortions of our being are eased gently through judgment,
the fierceness of your love is holding us upright,
the light of your eye shines with compassion and justice.

Dear God, we bring to you everything of which we are unaware, the
unknown murky devices of our fearful hearts, the untapped sources of
generosity and laughter, the forgotten confusions and hurts from which come
our excessive anger, the unrealised capacity for truth and forbearance.
Reveal us to ourselves and reassure us in the true humanity of Jesus Christ.

IN PRAISE OF GOD, ABUNDANT AND GENEROUS

Refrain: Let the people praise you, O God:
let all creation praise you.

We praise you dear God in your holy city,
we renew our vows in the holy places.
For you meet us in the depth of our being,
when we come to confess all that is true of us.
When our misdeeds haunt us with their power,
your generous love sweeps them aside.

Blessed are those whom you choose as your friends,
who lodge with you in your house.
You empower them with talents and gifts,
you crown them with an abundance of blessings.

In dread deeds you will deliver us,
O God of our salvation,
for you are the hope of the ends of the earth,
and of the distant seas.

By your strength you make the mountains rise,
by your power you gouge the valleys deep.
You still the raging of the seas,
the roaring of the waves,
and the tumult of the peoples.

Those who dwell at the ends of the earth
are held in awe at your wonders:
the dawn and the evening sing your praise.

You tend the earth and you water it,
you make it rich and fertile.
Your clouds are full of water,
they provide rain for the swelling grain.

Refrain: Let the people praise you, O God,
let all creation praise you.

You drench the furrows,
you level the ridges between,
you soften the soil with showers
and bless its early growth.
You refresh hearts withered and dry,
you bring to life the land parched with drought.

You crown our years with good gifts,
the fruit trees drip with abundance.
The alpine pastures shimmer with green,
the hills are wreathed with dancing clouds.
The meadows are clothed with sheep,
and the valleys mantled with corn.

Loving God, ceaselessly redeeming and creating, astonish us with your
abundant generosity, and still our hearts in awe and wonder.

SYMPHONY OF PRAISE

Refrain: Let the whole earth shout with joy to our God:
let all the people sing your praise.

Let the earth give praise to you, our Creator,
let all the peoples of the world give you praise.
Let psalms ring out to your glory,
for awesome indeed are your works.
Those who would defy you are brought low,
and the peoples fall silent in your presence.

Let the people you have redeemed give you praise:
marvellous are the deeds you have wrought for us.
You turned the waters into dry land,
and we passed through the sea on foot.
So we rejoiced in your strength:
your redeeming power has no end.
Even though the rebellious rise,
your quiet strength quells them.

Let the people you have rescued give you praise,
let the sound of singing voices carry far.
You established us where we now dwell,
you keep us from all lasting harm.
Yet you test us as silver is tried,
you catch us in the nets of our weaving,
you let others ride over us roughshod,
you lay sharp torment on our loins.
No easy wealth or worldly applause
as we go through fire and water!
But you have borne our pain with us,
bringing us into a place broad and free.

Refrain: Let the whole earth shout with joy to our God:
let all the people sing your praise.

I too will add my morsel of praise
as I thank you for all you have done.
I have kept my vows in the teeth of distress,
tempted to hold back my offering.
But I bring my best gifts to your presence,
my possessions and talents, all that is yours.
When I cherished evil you brought me low,
and turned my twisted heart to face you again.
You heard the deepest voice of my being,
fain as it was, unknown to my clamour,
and you responded with grace unpredictable,
you never ceased in your love and your care.

Let the wordless cries of creation, and the shaped voices of the people, let the
deep sighs of each heart and the testimony of faithful lips, let all be joined
in a harmony of exultant praise to you, Beloved God, our Creator and
Redeemer.

GOD'S ABUNDANT BLESSINGS

Refrain: Let the people praise you, O God,
let all the people praise you.

God be gracious to us and bless us,
and show us the light of your countenance
and be merciful to us,
that your way may be known on earth,
your saving health among all nations.

Let the nations rejoice and be glad,
for you judge the people with wisdom,
and you guide the nations upon earth.

Then shall the earth bring forth the harvest,
and God, even our own God, shall give us great blessing.
Dear God, you will bless us indeed,
and all the ends of the earth shall praise your holy name.

*O God of wise judgment, accepting us as we are and guiding us in your
ways, enable us so to appreciate your gifts of the harvest that we may know
them as a pledge of abundant life and thank you as the source and goal of all
that is good.*

WHAT KIND OF POWER?

Refrain: We praise you, O God, for your power,
         the power of the Way of Christ.

O God, humble and truthful,
scatter falsehood and bloated pride.
By the fierce light of your eyes
shrivel the power of the powers.
As smoke vanishes in the wind,
so shall they be dispersed.
As wax sizzles in the flame,
so shall evil squirm in your presence.
But justice and truth will be glad,
they will exult and rejoice.

We sing to you, O God,
we sing praise to your name.
We give you the glory
in the midst of our desert.
You come with living water
to dry and thirsty ground.
You are the father of the fatherless,
you are the mother of orphans,
you uphold the cause of the widow,
you give voice to the cries of the poor.
You give the desolate a home to dwell in,
you bring prisoners out of the dungeon.
Only those who complain and rebel,
who resent second place to the outcast,
know the storms of the desert within them,
feel the sun scorching their pride.

Like your people of old we delight in you,
glad of the home and the land which you give us,
which you put in our hands to care for.
Marching out as you do in the wilderness,
still leading us on by the pillar of fire,
you go on always before us,
preparing a place for your dwelling.
We bless you and give you thanks,
for you bear us as your burden.
You are to us a God who saves,
by your power we escape the pangs of death.

Even the snow-capped mountains shrink in your presence,
all the wealth of the nations is as nothing before you.
The power of the haughty is a broken reed,
our silver and gold worthless on your scales.
You quieten our shouts of triumph and victory,
as we see your rain refreshing our enemies.

Sing to God, O realms of earth,
sing praises to the God of the heavens,
who rides on the stormy wind,
whose voice thunders through the skies.
O God, you are awesome and terrible,
your light blinds even through clouds.
You give strength and power to your people,
to resist and scatter the relishers of war.

*Refrain: We praise you, O God, for your power,
the power of the Way of Christ.*

Exuberant is our victory song,
yet we are no better
than those who oppose us.
We too are greedy for spoil,
self-righteous in slaughter.
Let us see you again
as you came to us,
contracted to the span of a child,
helpless in the arms of his mother,
compassionate in bearing
while pinned to a cross,
taking the trampling of blood
deep in the heart of your being,
breaking the barrier of death
to new and glorious life.

We fall silent before the mystery of love,
this renouncing of power familiar so long,
this reversal of power that none can defeat,
this wonder we can scarcely believe.

*Dear God, as we struggle to understand and use the power aright that you
entrust to us, set before us again the way of Jesus, and work through us in
your Spirit, that we may steward our power in ways that do not bind others
but free them to take their share in the inheritance of life. May we grow not
tall but humble.*

ANY HOPE FOR THE EARTH?

Refrain: The earth and the people decay:
we breathe but a whisper of prayer.

Save us, O God: we are perishing!
The seas are swelling and flooding the land.
The rivers sweep away the soil laid bare,
the algae thickens off the summer coasts.

What is this weariness that grips us,
this cry of alarm that sticks in our throat,
the eye of conscience that no longer sees you,
the snap of hatred in those we thought wise?

We shame and disgrace our ancestors,
we betray those who come after us,
we rape the earth who mothered us,
we mock the few who stand for truth,
we have become as strangers to our children,
we are like aliens from a planet far away.

No longer is our word our bond;
we destroy trust by rumours and lies;
we find fault wherever we go,
we pillory those who are different.

We throw all the blame on to foreigners,
on to those in positions of power.
In truth there are few who are innocent,
the humble, the needy, the oppressed.
and vengeance is a luxury now.
The bombs and the guns of our fear
now destroy the earth and our neighbour.

In despair we are trapped and brought low,
unaware and unable to change.
We have even forgotten there may be a God,
a power beyond our own to whom we could cry.

Refrain: The earth and the people decay:
we breathe but a whisper of prayer.

In this our critical time,
is there a God who is good?
What price deliverance now,
as the very earth and the seas turn upon us?

Pride, greed, and malice all mock at us:
inordinate selfishness cries out in triumph.
With insults we break others' hearts,
we trample the weak to the ground.

We poison the food of our children,
the wine on our tables turns into vinegar.
We toss aside those we pretend we have loved,
our loins shake with disease.

The streets of our cities are deserted,
the rich and strong have flown to the hills.
The flowers of the parks turn to weeds,
the slides of the children rust.

We croak from the mire of the pit:
Let the echo of the walls be our prayer.
Let the menace of the waves turn to laughter.
Let the currents of the rivers dance.

From deep underground let the waters rise,
let them float us out of the caverns of darkness.
Let seeds of the trees be planted again,
let the clouds rain with pure water.

High on a cross a man hangs parched,
forsaken by friends and by God,
taking to himself their suffering and pain.
He dies with a cry – a whisper or howl? –
yet trusting the one who is absent.

Open our eyes again that we may see,
unfold our hearts to be open to your love.
May we greet our neighbours in trust,
and rebuild the walls of the city.

Be for us, O God, a deliverer still,
a God of compassion and joy.
Then will our mouths discover praise:
we will glorify you with thankful hearts.

As the sun returns to us in the depths of winter, come, O strange and terrible God, so often silent and hidden, rescue us from the brink of our doom, and renew the scarred face of the earth.

FAITH STRIPPED BARE

Refrain: Hold to the God who is absent,
trust in the God who withdraws.

The ruthless seek to destroy,
they hurt beyond repair.
Gaunt and hollow-eyed,
their victims limp to the grave.

Refused even their dignity,
they have no voice of their own.
Their faces press to the window,
they slink starving away.

The cruel are oblivious:
surely they would be appalled
by a conscience revived,
by eyes that were opened.

The cries of the needy are drowned
by their baying taunts of mockery.
Blind to the needs of the weak,
they dismiss them as merely a number.

The needy cry to the heavens,
to the Eagle with piercing eye.
But the skies are empty and cold,
no deliverer descends in our day.

Is there a God of compassion?
Is there a God of justice?
Is there One yearning in love?
Is there a God who can save?

Why do you delay your appearing?
Why do you keep us nailed to our pain?
Why do you harden the hearts of the cruel?
Why is our sense of you slipping away?

God, hard to believe in, bring us through dark nights of doubt to the joy in
which our ancestors danced your praise.

A PRAYER OF OLD AGE

Refrain: As the winds of winter gather,
do not forsake me, O God.

You have been the source of my strength, O God,
from before the day I was born.
You brought me forth from the womb,
you sustained me before ever I knew of you.
You were the confidence of my heedless youth,
you gave me my hope and my courage.

When I strove with the evil in my heart,
when I fought the enemies of your truth,
you refreshed me in the heat of the battle,
you were the rock in whose shade I recovered.
You were my stronghold on the mountain crag,
you were my refuge in the homes of my friends.

I have seen the eyes of the pitiless and cruel,
I have been wounded by words and by deeds.
I have been ignored and neglected by the powerful:
they pass over my name for promotion.
They have gossiped with glee at my failings,
they delight in rumour and lies.

My fate has filled many with awe:
I have become as a warning and portent.
And now I contend with old age,
withdrawing my eyes and my ears.
Few and grey are the hairs of my head –
no problem in numbering them now!

In this new testing of faith,
still would I praise you, my God.
I long for you still with hope,
and I will praise you more and more.
My mouth shall tell of your ways
to the generations taking my place.

Refrain: As the winds of winter gather,
do not forsake me, O God.

Yes, you have brought me through deep waters,
through trials bitter and troublesome.
You have burdened me yet given me strength,
you have raised me up from the depths.
Bless me now in the days of my fading,
turn to me again and give me your comfort.

Your just ways, O God, spread through the world –
great is the tale of your wonders.
I will make music in praise of your faithfulness,
through the days of my life and beyond.
I will sing of the mystery of Love,
my being soul-deep will rejoice in your name.

Even through the waters of death will you bring me,
keeping at bay my terror of drowning.
My lungs will fill with the breath of new life,
and I will praise you in the garden of delight.
We will dance as the poor enriched,
we will sing as the oppressed redeemed.

Those who knew not what they did,
and those who relished their malice,
even our enemies, through their shame and disgrace,
will be lured by the beauty of Love,
will weep at the music they spurned,
will at last speak the truth from their hearts.

As trust and doubt, distress and delight, success and failure, wax and wane
through the years, keep our eyes fixed on you, dear God, and give us courage
to face the trials and temptations that have yet to come our way.

A PRAYER FOR JUST AND WISE RULERS

Refrain: Give wisdom to those who govern,
who bear burdens on the people's behalf.

O God, give wisdom to those who govern us,
a sense of justice to those who wield power,
that they may frame laws that are life-giving,
that the poor and the weak may breathe freely.
May they defend the cause of the needy,
save the abandoned and orphans,
disarm the rebellious and violent.

May such wisdom endure like the sun and moon,
giving light from one age to the next.
May justice rain down like showers
that water the new-sown fields.
In our days may justice flourish,
and abundance of peace till the moon be no more.

May wisdom reign from sea to sea,
following the great rivers to the end of the earth.
May folly bow down to truth,
the enemies of justice lick the dust.
May all the rulers of the peoples seek wisdom,
the nations serve the ways of justice and truth.

Those who are wise deliver the needy when they call,
the weak and those who have no one to speak for them.
They will rescue them from oppression and violence,
and their lives are precious in their sight.

So may there be abundance of grain in the land,
to the tops of the hills may it wave.
Let the mountains be laden with peace,
with the prosperity that follows from justice.
May the corn swell with the gentle rains,
the sheaves thicken like the grass of the meadows.

Refrain: Give wisdom to those who govern,
who bear burdens on the people's behalf.

May prayer be made for those in high office,
that they may bear their burdens with wisdom.
May blessings be invoked on them day by day,
may they be heartened by the prayers of the people.

Blessed be the God of all the earth,
who alone is all wisdom and justice,
who alone does great wonders.
Blessed be the glorious name of God:
may the universe be filled with God's glory.
Let the Amen echo with praise.

O God, the cry of our prayer and the reality of our politics are far apart.
Renew in all of us a thirst for justice, a cherishing of the earth and the
oceans, the wisdom of restraint, and a deep desire for the common good.

PERPLEXITY UNRESOLVED BUT TRANSFORMED

Refrain: Let us delve the deepest questions,
living their mystery.

To the loyal and loving and faithful,
God indeed is pure goodness.
And yet I was losing my foothold,
slipping and slithering from faith.
For I was envious of the boast of sinners:
without God they were entirely content.

They suffer no pains that I can see:
they look ever so healthy and sleek.
They never seem plunged into grief,
never harassed or thrown off course.
Pride is the signet ring on their finger,
craving for power fits them like a glove.

Their eyes gleam through folds of fat,
mirror of their empty minds.
Their faces ooze malice and greed,
their hearts brim over with the basest of thoughts,
with mocking laughter and cynical scorn,
overwhelming with menace and threats.
Their slanders are raised against heaven,
their tongue plies to and fro on the earth.

Of course they carry the mob with them,
lapping up their words like cheap wine –
What has God to do with us?
Are you still there?
Do you take any notice?
They go their godless way with a will,
untroubled they grow ever more wealthy.

Why did I ever keep faith with you,
why did I keep my conscience alert?
Every day is a punishment to me,
every morning I wake feeling beaten.

Refrain: Let us delve the deepest questions,
          living their mystery.

I have often thought, Do like those others.
But then I would have betrayed the Body of Christ,
I would have denied the faith of my ancestors.
So I was tossed backwards and forwards,
perplexed, desperate, baffled by it all.

Then I turned to worship you, O God,
and I pierced the heart of the mystery.
I began to see you with a sword in your side,
I began to see life in the light of your future.

The life of the unheeding totters on quicksand,
keeling over and falling to ruin.
They are in one fell moment destroyed.
They are living in the shadow of nightmares,
evil dreams that haunt in the morning,
dreams that are suddenly ended,
as they fall to their doom, unmourned and forgotten.

Yes, the struggle for faith has cost me dear:
like Jacob I limp in the sunrise.
With the heart's blood alone is victory wrought,
the price of the whole of my being.
You have embraced me in the ocean wastes,
a bird whose wings are trapped in black oil.
You weave all my doubts and distress
to a pattern of dancing joy.

It was a bitter heart that made me rebellious,
I was hurt in the depth of my being.
Distraught, I hammered away at you:
deranged, I vented my fury.
Nevertheless you absorbed my rage,
you embraced me and held me,
drawing the poision out of my heart,
giving me rest and deep peace.

I do not see you, yet do I trust in you.
No wisdom or strength dare I claim as my own.
Yet still you uphold me, and receive me in glory.

Though my flesh is falling apart,
though my heart is strained to breaking,
though my bones ache in the winter,
though my blood runs thin in my veins,
nevertheless still you are God,
you are the future that waits for me,
How this can be is hidden from me,
you are the mystery giving no answers.
Yet I look to no one else in the universe,
with you I am well content.

Those who abandon you are doomed.
To break faith with you is to be lost.
True joy lies in drawing closer to God,
to the suffering, the mystery, the terrible love.
In you I believe that all shall be well.
So I will speak of your name and your ways,
not with a shouting that covers my doubts,
but a whisper sounding the depths of enduring.

*And yes, the questions trouble us still, perplexing God, and will do so to the
end of our days. Is there no way the pride of the powerful can be punctured?
Can we not learn to share the good things of the earth? Do we not collude
with those who are unjust? Do we not compensate too glibly with the
promise of good things after death? Nevertheless, nevertheless... So in the
midst of our questions, deepen our trust; in the midst of our trust, keep our
questions alive. Cleanse the eye of our perception and purify our hearts that
we may will one thing, that your way indeed be followed through and beyond
the perplexities we cannot escape. Glorify your name, O God, and justify
your ways!*

THE SEA OF FAITH?

Refrain: The tide of faith still ebbs:
Dare we work and wait for its turning?

The more we are aware, O God,
the harder does faith become.
The more we contemplate the desolation,
the further you seem to withdraw.

Millions die in the labour camps,
a child's scream pierces the night.
The chainsaws screech through the forests,
an elm withers in the meadow.

The desert sands creep onward,
acid rain crumbles the statues,
chemicals choke the rivers and lakes,
nuclear waste stores wrath in the earth.

Beautiful buildings decay into ruin,
exquisite carvings crumble to dust.
The places of prayer are too heavy for faith,
their very doors oppressive with weight.

You have deserted the altars, O God,
the faithful few ignore their decadence,
maintaining at extraordinary expense
that from which the meaning has departed.

Faith retreats into privacies,
or clashes with violent fervour.
The sensitive shudder and whisper,
the bullies shout and trample.

The grass of the arenas is scarred,
games turn to battles, the injured hobble.
New domes rise up from industrial waste,
temples for consumers at worship.

The voice of the prophet is thrown to the wind,
the springs of sacrifice run dry.
Service of others is measured by money,
those who would guide lack all sense of direction.

The tales of our faith falter,
the memory of God grows dim.
Did you really swoop down to rescue,
do you truly care for Jerusalem?

Did your hand strike the rocks of the desert,
and make the water flow?
Do you care for the sparrows' brood?
Do you give us manna in our wilderness?

Look on this earth of your creating,
see the billowing clouds of corruption,
listen to the trudge of the weary,
open your ears to the taunts of the mindless.

Dare we praise you, O God, do you hear our cry,
meeting it in the depths of your being,
giving yourself for us and all people,
the Lamb slain across aeons of time?

To the mystery of the Cross we hurl our questions,
and doggedly worry away at our doubts.
Yes, you absorb the wastes of our wraths and sorrows,
turning pain to glory in the vortex of Love.

*O God, fading from our sight as our own sight grows dim, work still in us
and through your world, till our eyes open to a strange and shocking light,
a scarcely believable new dawn.*

SURE JUDGMENT

Refrain: Come with the judgment that chastens,
come with the wounds that heal.

Love flashes like lightning,
cuts through the heart of evil,
shows up pride in its ghastly light,
surprises our hidden boasting.

Love thunders in judgment,
sounding from horizon to horizon,
searching the depths of our being,
proclaiming the truth from the rooftops.

In awe and wonder we look to you,
O God, creating anew through your judgment,
sovereign and free in discernment,
at last making things right.

You hold a strange cup in your hands,
foaming with wine, astringent with spices.
You give it to us to drink,
to test the extent of our wickedness.
We drain it down to the dregs,
and see ourselves as we are.

The wine like liquid flame
burns through the layers of evil.
Like a hammer to the skull,
it breaks the crusts of habit.

Drained of our evil we tremble,
empty and naked before you.
We would be glad of the rags of the starving,
so defenceless do we feel.

The oppressed and the dying look into our eyes,
stretch out their hands in their weakness,
not to receive – we have nothing –
but to lift us out of fear and despair.

In them do we see you, O Christ,
eyes so clear and compassionate,
forgiving our wrong at the cost of your life,
with wounded palms embracing us.

We praise you, dear God,
we give you the glory.
We will tell of your wonders,
of your judgment and mercy.

Living Flame, refine us in the truth, burn out all that is impure with the fiery eye of clarity, and warm into life the frozen battered child that longs to live again.

THE LION'S WRATH

*Refrain: With dread deeds save us,
with wrath embrace us.*

Heraldic you stand on the battlements,
radiant in the dawn of the day –
Lion of Judah, powerful and just,
more majestic than snow-capped mountains.

Jerusalem you claim as your own,
scattering the haughty and proud,
at a stroke snapping their arrows,
silencing their rebellion with a roar.

The men of war tremble,
there is no strength in their arms;
they stand aghast, helpless;
dumbfounded, they cannot speak.

You beat our swords into ploughshares,
you defeat all the wiles of our warring,
you terrify those who use terror,
the powerless and oppressed have nothing to fear.

Our human wraths hurt and destroy:
your wrath is clear in its justice,
a terrible love that drums in our ears,
insistent, compelling, triumphant.

Awesome is your promise to love us,
terrifying is the response you seek from us.
Our weapons of war lie broken before you:
your vow is fulfilled in our sight.

*Lion of Wrath, we would cower from the prowling of your love, we would
slink into the prison we have made for ourselves. Give us your courage to face
our fear, break down our iron bars, in one bound rescue us despite ourselves.*

PAST MERCIES, PRESENT DESPAIR, FUTURE HOPE

Refrain: Keep the memory of your goodness alive,
fan into flame the embers of hope.

In anxiety I murmur towards you,
in distress I cry out from my heart.
I call but hear only my echo:
Is God wrapped in silence for ever?
My eyes stream tears of sorrow,
groaning wells up from within.
Despair grips my heart like ice,
there is no breath in my lungs.

Drenched in sweat I lie on my bed,
in the grip of delirium and fever.
There is nothing to cool me and comfort,
a terrible darkness descends.
I stretch out my hands and my soul,
yearning towards you from the depth of the night.
I think on your name but see nothing:
exhausted, my spirit faints.

Disconsolate, I pluck at the strings,
unable to hear the music we made,
eye to eye loving each other,
with melody in our hearts.
Paralyzed in terror, my eyes stare wild:
gripped by fear, I am weighted to the ground.
Like a rabbit dazzled by headlamps
I am dazed and cannot flee.

Will you cast me away for ever?
Will you no longer surprise me with joy?
Is your mercy vanished for ever?
Have your promises come to end?

Refrain: Keep the memory of your goodness alive,
fan into flame the embers of hope.

Have you forgotten to be gracious?
Have you closed your heart to pity?
Have you broken that strong right arm?
Has your love no power to endure?

I suffer a sickness of soul:
I demand you live up to my image.
You are no idol to serve my desires:
Thou art Thou, living, mysterious, and free.
With numbed fingers I hold on to you yet,
like a climber on the face of a mountain.
Though the waves of the sea crash over me,
like a limpet I cling to the rock.

Dogged and grim, yet I remember the past,
the wonders of rescue, the God who acts.
I will think on the deeds you have done,
I will meditate on the God who acts.
You made known your power among the peoples,
by great deeds you redeemed your own.
You brought the children of Jacob and Joseph
from bondage to the promise of freedom.

The waters of the sea cowered back before you,
the voice of your thunder was heard in the whirlwind,
your lightning lit up the horizon,
the clouds poured down rain at your bidding.
Your path was through the Sea of Reeds,
and on through the trackless wastes.
The earth shuddered at your passing,
though your footsteps were not seen.

By the hand of Moses and Aaron,
you led your people out of slavery.
By the wounds of your Beloved on the Cross,
you led them through the pangs of death.

In times of exhaustion you lifted us up,
through closed doors you surprised us with joy.
Through the words of friends you have encouraged us,
through intimate touch you come close again.
And yes, you are holy indeed,
leading us beyond all that comforts us.
Of course we must expect not to see you
when you leave no trace of your passing.

Narrow is the path, no room for another,
thin is the air, no breath to name you,
thick is the cloud, there is nothing we can see,
lonely is the way, no companions now.
Veiled in mystery, yet you are God.
Dark is the night, yet your glory transforms it.
Revealed in Jesus, yet a stranger so often.
The Unknown That Shalt Be, yet the hope of our future.

*O God, the same yesterday, today, and for ever, though we sense your
absence in a bleak despairing time, focus our minds and hearts on memories
of grace surprising us, that faith may be kept alive and hope re-kindled.*

RIDDLES OF HISTORY

Refrain: Deluded, rebellious, estranged,
we know neither ourselves nor our God,
the God whose ways are mysterious,
an enigma, a question, a riddle.

Listen to my teaching, O my people:
incline your ears to the words of my mouth.
For I will open my lips in a parable,
and expound the mysteries of former times.
What we have heard and known,
all that our ancestors told us,
we will not hide from our children,
but declare to a generation to come:
the praiseworthy acts of God,
God's mighty and wonderful works.
O God, you established a law for your people,
you witnessed to your ways in Israel,
which you commanded our ancestors
to teach to their children,
that future generations might know you,
and children yet to be born,
that they in their turn might teach it
that their daughters and sons might trust you,
that they might keep your commandments
and not forget your works –
as did their ancestors,
a rebellious and stubborn generation,
a generation whose heart was warped,
whose spirit was not faithful to God.   *Refrain*

The children of Ephraim armed with the bow
turned back in the day of their battle.
They did not keep your covenant, O God,
they refused to walk in your law:
they forgot what you had done,
and the wonders you had shown them.
You worked marvels in the sight of their forebears,
in the land of Egypt, in the country of Zoan.
You divided the sea and let them pass,
you made the waters pile up in a heap.
In the daytime you led them with a cloud,
and all night long with the pillar of fire.
You cleft rocks in the wilderness,
and gave them drink in abundance.
You made streams flow out of the rock,
you caused the waters to tumble like rivers.
But for all this they sinned against you,
and rebelled against their God in the desert.   *Refrain*

They wilfully put you to the test,
and demanded food for their appetite.
They spoke against you and said,
"Can you prepare a table in the wilderness?
You indeed struck the rock and the waters flowed,
but can you also give bread and meat for your people?"
When you heard it you were angry
and a fire was kindled against Jacob,
your wrath blazing against Israel.
For they put no trust in you,
nor would they believe your power to save.
Then you commanded the clouds above,
and opened the doors of heaven.
You rained down manna for them to eat,
and gave them the bread of heaven.
Mere mortals ate the food of angels,
which you gave to them in abundance.
You stirred up the south east wind
and guided it by your power.

Refrain: *Deluded, rebellious, estranged,*
we know neither ourselves nor our God,
the God whose ways are mysterious,
an enigma, a question, a riddle.

You rained down meat on them thick as dust,
and winged birds like the sands of the sea.
You made them fall into the midst of their camp,
and all about their tents.
So they ate and were well filled,
for you had given them what they desired.
But before they had satisfied their craving,
while the food was still in their mouths,
your anger blazed up against them
and you slew their strongest men
and laid low the youth of Israel.   *Refrain*

But for all this they sinned yet more
and put no faith in your wonders.
So you ended their days like a breath,
and their years with sudden terror.
When you struck them down then they sought you,
they turned and searched eagerly for their God.
They remembered that God was their rock,
their strength and their redeemer.
But they lied to you with their mouths,
and dissembled with their tongues,
for their hearts were not fixed upon you,
nor were they true to your covenant.
Yet being merciful you forgave their iniquity,
and withheld your hand from destroying them.
Many times you turned your anger aside
and would not wholly arouse your fury.
You remembered that they were but flesh,
like a wind that passes and does not return.   *Refrain*

How often they grieved you in the wilderness,
and rebelled against you in the desert.
Again and again they put you to the test
and provoked you, O Holy One of Israel.

They did not remember your power,
or the day when you rescued them,
how you wrought your signs in Egypt,
your wonders in the country of Zoan.
For you turned their rivers into blood,
so that they could not drink from the streams.
You sent swarms of flies that devoured them,
and frogs that laid them waste.
You gave their crops to the locust,
and the fruits of their labours to the grasshopper.
You struck down their vines with hailstones,
and their sycamore trees with frost.
You gave up their cattle to the hail,
and their flocks to the flash of the lightning.
You loosed on them a terrible anger,
a fierce indignation, your distress and your fury.
You would not spare them from death
but gave up their lives to the pestilence.
You struck down the firstborn of Egypt,
the firstfruits of the womb in the dwelling of Ham.

Refrain

As for your own people you led them out like sheep,
and guided them in the wilderness like a flock.
You led them to safety and they were not afraid,
but the sea overwhelmed their enemies.
You brought them to the land of the promise,
to the mountains your right hand had won.
You drove out the tribes before you
and gave their lands to your people.
You settled the tribes of Israel in their tents.
But they rebelled against you, O God of deliverance,
and put you to the test:
they would not obey your Commandments.
They turned back and were treacherous again,
they turned aside, slack as an unstrung bow.
They provoked you to anger at heathen shrines,
moved you to jealousy with their carved idols.

Refrain: Deluded, rebellious, estranged,
we know neither ourselves nor our God,
the God whose ways are mysterious,
an enigma, a question, a riddle.

You heard and were angry, you utterly rejected them,
you forsook the tabernacle at Shiloh,
the tent where you dwelt among the people.
You gave the ark of your power into captivity,
your glory into the hands of the enemy.
You delivered your people to the sword,
and were enraged against them.
Fire devoured the young men,
there was no one to bewail the young women,
Their priests fell by the sword,
and there was none to mourn for the widows.   *Refrain*

Then, O God, you awoke from sleep,
like a warrior inflamed with wine.
You struck the backsides of your enemies,
bringing them down to their shame.
You rejected the family of Joseph,
you refused the tribe of Ephraim.
But you chose the tribe of Judah,
and the hill of Zion which you loved.
You built the sanctuary high as the heavens,
and as firm as the earth which you founded.
You chose David the youngest as your servant,
and plucked him away from the sheepfold.
You took him from guiding the flocks,
to be the shepherd of your people Jacob,
and of Israel your own possession.
He tended them with a true and faithful heart,
and guided them with skilful hands.   *Refrain*

And so the story unfolded,
the mystery ever deepening,
a kingdom split apart,
a people carried off into exile.
Even the clue of the Cross
has left us many a puzzle.
Our loyalty ebbs and flows,
our sense of your presence too.
Those in high office betray you,
integrity crumbles in gossip.
The obscure are so often submerged,
the powerful far beyond love.
The stones of the churches decay,
your agelong Spirit moves on.
We have become so timid and fearful,
we refuse to enter the unknown.
We desperately cling to our comforts,
one by one you take them away.
We resent you stripping us bare,
untrusting of this prelude to glory.   *Refrain*

*Mysterious God, choosing the small, the unnoticed, the obscure, to renew
the way of your covenant when your followers wander and fail you, strive
yet with our intractable clay; open us to the love you revealed to us in Jesus
Christ, emptied of power, untouched by illusion, dying unrecognized, yet
for those with eyes to see the decisive clue to the mystery of your being.*

THE BODY OF GOD

Refrain: O God, we wound your body:
come quickly, heal and save us.

We neglect, we ravage the body.
We rape the earth, your temple.
We pollute the rivers, the oceans.
We care not for the soil that sustains us.
And the earth cries out in pain.
The algae fills the creeks,
sucking down the unwary,
releasing its poisonous fumes.

We neglect, we ravage the body.
We take our pleasures with violence.
We forget the language of reverence.
We care not for the weak and the vulnerable.
And the people cry out in pain.
Their anger rises in vengeance:
they pass on the needles infected,
they delight in spreading disease.

We neglect, we ravage the body.
We flatten the beautiful cities.
We ransack the places of prayer.
We care not for beauty, for peace.
And the land cries out in pain.
The contorted ruins smoulder.
The survivors stumble in shock,
their children inherit their wounds.

We neglect, we ravage the body.
Radiation drifts on the wind.
Waste is dumped in the oceans.
We care not for fish or for bird.
And the trees cry out in pain,
sprouting mis-shapen leaves.
An earthquake in the depths of the seas
splits open the canisters of doom.

O God, forgive our murderous deeds and blind, unthinking rage. Give us your Spirit of compassionate anger, that we may live and work in harmony with you for the healing of the body of this planet, gasping for air, sores weeping on its skin. Make us a people of one earth, loved and cherished as bodies should.

THE FACE OF GOD

Refrain: Light of the Spirit shine on us;
Face of Glory transfigure us;
Eyes of Christ restore us.

Radiant and glorious God,
shining through the universe,
lighting our tortuous landscape,
guiding your troublesome peoples,
straighten the path of your coming,
stride forth to meet us and save us.

Radiant and glorious God,
shining through a human face,
illuminate our blinded eyes,   ʿ ι
guide us with an inner light,
feed us who gasp by the wayside,
lift us up with nurturing hand.

We have misused the freedom you gave us,
we have felt the anger of your love.
You have fed us with the bread of tears,
and given us many a bitter drink.

You cared for us like a young vine,
clearing the ground and planting us in.
You nourished the soil for our roots to deepen,
you sent us the warmth of the sun and the rain.
We flourished and grew strong,
our boughs were like those of the cedar.
Our branches stretched out to the sea,
our tender shoots to the great river.

Why then have you sent us drought?
Why do the locusts devour our fruit?
Why does the wind tear our branches?
Why do the boars of the forest uproot us?
O God, no longer do we see your face,
no longer do we hear your voice.

With the eye of your compassion look upon us.
Prune us if need be, but do not destroy.
We are a fickle and cowardly people:
strengthen our wills and heal our wounds.
Let all that is wilful in us perish at your word,
let all that is slothful be burned.
Empower us again to follow your way,
give us life and we shall delight in your name.

Living God, whose face no one can look upon and live, sustain our faith in the human face of Christ revealing the infinite depths of your justice and compassion. So shine upon us with the light of your Spirit that we may recognize you in the faces of one another and realize the presence of your glory among us.

THE GOD WHO YEARNS TO SAVE

Refrain: O God who saved a small people
from slavery, oppression, and fear,
deliver the peoples of earth
from our imprisonments one of another.

The people of God sang for joy,
the people of the God of Jacob.
They beat the drum,
they plucked the strings,
they blew the horn of the ram,
and the people gathered.
At the phases of the moon
they held their festival,
even as their ancestors
from their time in Egypt.

God spoke to the people in a voice not known:
I eased your shoulders of burdens,
your hands were freed from the load.
You called to me and I rescued you,
I answered from the place of secret thunder,
I tested you at the waters of Meribah.

My people, listen to my charge.
Israel, if only you would hear me!
Do not bow down to alien gods,
let there be no strange gods among you.
I am your God and your Saviour,
who brought you out of the land of Egypt.
Open your mouth wide and I will satisfy you:
filled with my presence you will live in my truth.

But you would not listen to my voice,
you would have nothing to do with me.
So I gave you up to your stubborn hearts,
to walk according to your own designs.
If only you would listen to me,
if only you would walk in my ways.
I would soon defeat your enemies,
and lift you free of your oppressors.
Those who despise me would cringe before me,
they would be trapped in their fate for ever.
But I would feed you with the finest wheat,
with honey from the rock I would satisfy you.

Like our ancestors, O God, we would worship you,
we would be glad and sing for joy.
To us as to them you would speak,
reminding us of your yearning and care.
In the moment of prayer we are one with them,
our past is alive and so is the future.
You would warn and admonish us still,
for we also wander from your way.
We lay burdens upon one another:
oppressed, we oppress in our turn.
Spring the traps we have laid,
deliver us from the compulsion to punish.
Do not imprison us for ever,
even those we see as our enemies.

Do not exalt us who are far from deserving it,
at the expense of hell for our enemies.
The people of earth are your people now.
Work in us all your deeds of deliverance,
even in those who abuse and enslave,
in those who traffic in terror or drugs,
in those who dictate the slaughter of innocents.
If they are so thoroughly wicked,
that they dissolve into dust at your sight,
so let it be, your design come to nothing.
But would not your love then have failed?
Inscrutable God, is that not so?

Dear God, your heart yearns with longing for us to realize how trapped we are. You give us the freedom to choose to be imprisoned for ever. Yet your love with insistence compels. Turn our hearts and wills without our knowing it, and kindle in us the desire for true freedom. Deliver us in love's most costly way, and give us the courage to bear it, in Jesus, for whom such love was the weight of glory.

THE IDLE PROMISES OF IDOLS

Refrain: Down to the dust, vain idols!
Come, living God of justice.

They seem to be as gods,
those who promise utopias.
Fickle as a crowd we gawp,
cheering the latest idolatry:
Romantic illusions of singers,
false pledges of politicians,
slippery words of the gurus,
sleek suits of the televangelists.

From your pedestals you no longer see,
high above the weak and oppressed.
You say nothing about the orphaned and widowed,
never touch the lives of the silenced.
You say nothing of the toughness of love,
you promise no just laws for the poor,
your words pass over the stricken,
your mouthings stir up irrational guilt.

You proclaim a false god of terror,
by threats you hold on to your power,
you never show the true God,
wounded by love, embracing the failure.
Indeed you are lost, you crumble,
you wander about in the darkness,
you stumble, you do not understand,
your name will vanish into dust.

O God, make your promises true,
imbue us with your Spirit of justice.
Favour the oppressed, humble the oppressor,
bring laughter and love to our eyes.

*O God, living God, if you are the living God, justify your ways to your
people, and let not our cry for justice echo in silence. We cling to our trust
in your promises. Fulfil them. Do not betray us. Do not be to us a false god.*

THE ENEMIES OF GOD

Refrain: Redeem your enemies, O God,
those who misuse your power.
Transform us all by your presence,
a power made holy by love.

A small people, in a small land,
surrounded by tribes that were hostile,
threatened by empires expanding,
cried out to their God to protect them.
Their enemies made their alliances,
whispering, conspiring, plotting together.
They schemed against those whom God cherished,
they seized on the pastures of God.

Who are your enemies now, O God?
A people apathetic who do not care,
those who sit at ease while millions slave,
those who eat their fill while children starve.
And those who wage war in the name of their God,
and those who supply them with weapons;
those who poison the rivers and seas,
and those who spread lies through our minds.

Destroy them, O God, who poison the land,
let their remains become dung for the earth.
Make them like chaff before the wind,
as insubstantial as thistledown.
May they cower backwards in fear,
flattened by the fury of your wind,
shrivelled by the heat of your fire,
the flame that sets hillsides ablaze.
Let them be disgraced and dismayed for ever,
and those who collude – like ourselves.
Wild-eyed, bewildered, let us tremble,
in a moment of dread and of truth.

Refrain: Redeem your enemies, O God,
those who misuse your power.
Transform us all by your presence,
a power made holy by love.

Yes, we yearn for the omnipotent king,
the ruler who gives life to the people,
who leads out his armies to lay waste and destroy.
Such a king was an ikon of God,
but the King on a Cross shows a power that is humbling,
an awesome love that endures through the pain,
that takes our rage and our venom to heart,
all of us guilty together.

May we turn from our hatreds and face you,
burned clean by the eye of your love,
that you may forgive our destruction and greed,
and our naming of strangers as enemies.
In your Spirit let us care for the earth,
in compassion one for another.
Let us welcome the strangers and share what we have,
enjoying the wealth of justice and friendship.

O God, ease our paranoia from our hearts, grown cold in this time of fear.
Remind us of the truth that even those who terrify us — eyes harsh and
vengeful — are created and loved by you. Show us how to be reconciled and
so to live in peace.

ON PILGRIMAGE

Refrain: The end is known in the midst of the journey:
the fulfilment is beyond our imagining.

How lovely are your dwellings, O God,
how beautiful are the holy places.
In the days of my pilgrimage I yearn for them:
they are the temples of your living presence.
√ I have a desire and longing to enter my true home:
my heart and my flesh rejoice in the living God.

For the sparrow has found a house for herself,
and the swallow a nest to lay her young.
Even so are those who dwell in your house –
they will always be praising you.
And your Spirit makes a home deep within us:
let us welcome and delight in your Presence.

Blessed are those whose strength is in you,
in whose heart are your ways,
who trudging through the plains of misery
find in them an unexpected spring,
a well from deep below the barren ground,
and the pools are filled with water.

They become springs of healing for others,
reservoirs of compassion to those who are bruised.
Strengthened themselves they lend courage to others,
and God will be there at the end of their journey.

O God of our ancestors, hear my prayer:
guide me as you did your servants of old.
Bless those who govern on the people's behalf,
keep us close to your will and your ways.

Refrain: The end is known in the midst of the journey:
the fulfilment is beyond our imagining.

One day lived in your presence
is better than a thousand in my own dwelling.
I had rather beg in the burning sun
on the threshold of the house of my God
than sit in cool courtyards
of luxury and worldly success.

For you are my light and my shield,
you will give me your grace and your glory.
You are ready with bountiful gifts,
overflowing to those who follow you.

Living God of love,
blessed are those who put their trust in you.

O God of the desert pilgrims, we who are wearied by monotonous days in
the sun, who are battered by the monstrous whirling winds, surprise us yet
with a monstrance of wonder, a revelation of love, an oasis of refreshment,
a taste of the harvest, a moment of grace.

ROOTED IN ONE LAND?

*Refrain: May we cherish the land of our birth,
and be rooted in the Earth and in God.*

We thank you, O God, for the land of our birth,
for a country to cherish and honour,
for farms and cities to care for,
gardens and houses to dwell in.

You chose a particular people,
you gave land to a wandering tribe,
that they might learn to follow your way,
and give light to the nations around them.

So often that light was dimmed by their sin,
as they turned aside from your path.
You led them through the mourning of exile,
and they knew you as Lord of the Earth.

Then you filled the life of one particular man,
born of your people, brought up in that land,
whose name has spread all over the earth,
calling us all to be neighbours.

Still does your love strive with our waywardness,
reaching across the abyss that is wrath,
opening our eyes to the needs of the hidden ones,
compelling us to cherish an earth that is fragile.

We look upon the world and its peoples,
and there seem few grounds for our faith.
We turn our hearts towards the Ground of our being,
and you meet us with riches of grace.

So you give us life yet again,
and we your people sing and rejoice,
speaking your praise on behalf of the creatures,
claiming our inheritance as stewards of Earth.

Refrain: May we cherish the land of our birth,
and be rooted in the Earth and in God.

Indeed you will speak peace to your people,
to your faithful ones who have turned their hearts.
Truly your salvation is near those who fear you,
and your glory will shine on our earth.

Mercy and truth have met together,
righteousness and peace have kissed each other.
Faithfulness will spring up from the earth,
and justice leap to meet it from heaven.

O God, you will give us all that is good,
and our lands will yield their plenty.
For righteousness will go before you,
and clear the way for your appearing.

God of the whole earth and God of each land, so guide us in your Spirit that
we may not betray our country for the sake of fanatical ideals, nor betray our
earth out of fearful and blinkered loyalties, through Jesus Christ the Just.

GOD IS GOD

*Refrain: Persistent in faithfulness,
constant in love.*

Like the sun through the heavens,
and the moon through its phases,
like the rivers that flow,
and the seas that welcome them,
so are you, God of the universe,

Like the humble of heart,
and the kindly of soul,
like the ones who forgive
and are no longer bitter,
so are you, God of compassion,

You hear the cry of the afflicted,
you listen to the howl of the lonely,
you continually search for the lost,
you heal the hurts of the wounded,
for you are a God of yearning,

You gladden the human heart,
you lift the burdens of the depressed,
you give new hope to the despairing,
you reach to the depths of the grave,
for you are a God of rejoicing,

You bind the rebellious,
you quieten the strident,
you draw the fangs of the ruthless,
you silence the bullying dictators,
for you are a God of justice,

You welcome the stranger,
you embrace the outcast,
you bear our pain,
you strive with our evil,
for you are a God crucified and risen,

Refrain: Persistent in faithfulness,
constant in love.

Abiding is your love,
enduring is your patience,
everlasting are your truths,
eternal, is your glory,
O God, you are God.

God of mystery and revelation, at the extremes of our distress and despair,
when you are the only hope left, let us hear your name again, and so take
courage on the journey:

I Am Who I Am,
I Shall Be Who I Shall Be,
That Which I Am I Shall Be,
That Which I Shall Be I Am.

I shall be there as the one who I there shall be,
I am with you always as I always choose to be with you.

I shall be there in the encounter
you cannot predict,
but there you will meet me,
and I shall be for you
as the one who there shall be.

CITIES OF PILGRIMAGE

Refrain: Lured by the God whose greatness is Love,
we draw near to the gates of the City.

Egypt, the old enslaver,
Babylon, the ancient foe,
Philistines over the border,
Phoenicians from the shores of the sea,
Ethiopians from over the mountains,
those who once were our enemies
now worship God in Jerusalem.

The eye of faith looks to the dawn,
to the day of peace universal,
to a new age of the salvation of God,
to an earth transfigured, made new.
The dancers dance; the singers make melody;
the fountains of God enliven the City.

The peoples are widely scattered
over the earth and across the sea.
A poet with vision broods
as the pilgrims draw near to Jerusalem,
to the God who draws them together
to give praise on the holy mountain.

The peoples of another time,
citizens of far-flung cities,
the powerful of Washington,
of Moscow and Beijing,
the weak of Sao Paulo,
of Soweto and Calcutta,
all the peoples give you praise.

Refrain: Lured by the God whose greatness is Love,
we draw near to the gates of the city.

Pilgrims to Jerusalem,
to Mecca and to Rome:
Faithful of Canterbury,
of Geneva and Byzantium:
Gatherers to the rivers,
to the Naranjara and the Ganges:
Markers of the journey
through the deserts and the mountains:
they celebrate in gratitude,
in wonder and rejoicing.

No room for the aloof and arrogant,
for the divisive and superior spirit:
God is greater than the idols of nations,
deeper in mystery than any faith.
Like a people of old, small, obscure,
stretched beyond fear to a wider belief,
so are God's people today
challenged by a love that is awesome,
drawn to the gates of the city of God,
whose name is yet to be known.

Living God, greater than the human heart, greater than all the peoples of the
world, greater than the faiths that try to cage you, shatter the idols which we
make to keep us safe, to claim you for ourselves, to portray you in superior
ways. Humble us, living God, and draw us by the magnet of your Love into
the glory of your Presence and the harmony of a new Jerusalem.

IN BLEAK DESPAIR

Refrain: There is drought in the depths of my being,
no rain, no water, no life.

The praise of your salvation, O God,
has died on lips that are parched.
The story of your wonders towards us
has turned hollow, bitter, and sour.
I doubt any prayer can enter your heart,
your ear is deaf to my cry.

Soul-deep I am full of troubles,
and my life draws near to the grave.
I totter on the edge of the abyss,
ghostly, ghastly, shrivelled.
I am like the wounded in war that stagger,
like a corpse strewn out on the battlefield.

I belong no more to my people,
I am cut off from your presence, O God.
You have put me in the lowest of dungeons,
in a pit of scurrying rats.
To a wall that drips with water I am chained,
my feet sink into mud.

I feel nothing but your pounding in my head,
surges of pain overwhelm me.
I cannot endure this suffering,
this furious onslaught, so searing.
I can remember no time without terror,
without turmoil and trouble of mind.

I have been dying since the day of my birth:
O God, have I ever really existed?
I have never known who I am,
and even my friends who once loved me,
who gave me some sense of belonging,
have drawn back in horror and left me.

*Refrain: There is drought in the depths of my being,
no rain, no water, no life.*

My sight fails me because of my trouble;
there is no light in the place of deep dark.
I am alone, bewildered, and lost;
yet I cannot abandon you, God.
Day after day I cry out to you,
early in the morning I pray in your absence.

Do you work wonders among the tombs?
Shall the dead rise up and praise you?
Will your lovingkindness reach to the grave,
your faithfulness to the place of destruction?
Are the stories of old an illusion?
Will you again do what is right in the land?

.

*In times of despair, O God, rain showers of gentleness upon us, that we may
be kindly one to another and also to ourselves. Renew in us the spirit of hope.
Even in the depths of the darkness, may we hear the approach of the One who
harrows hell and greets even Judas with a kiss.*

THE PROMISE

Refrain: The promises of God stand for ever:
when will we see them fulfilled?

We cannot know the depths of your being, O God,
you are to us a mystery profound.
Revealed as a love that is selfless,
still do we touch but a fringe of your being.
Your promises of love are steady and sure,
and yet in perplexity we doubt them.

Your people of old called you king of high heaven:
they thought of you praised by the holy ones,
by the inner council who held you in awe,
who praised your wonders and deeds.
They bowed down to the king who was just,
whose promises were very sure.
Justice was the foundation of your reign,
lovingkindness and faithfulness your closest attendants.

They praised you as the God of Power:
no-one could stand in the way of your purpose.
In strength and faithfulness and glory
you ruled the powers of creation.
You stilled the surging of the sea,
you reined in the monsters of chaos.
When the floods drowned out our wickedness,
you promised to withhold your destruction.

Your promises reached out to a particular people,
you gave them a land of their own.
You rescued them from slavery in Egypt,
and brought them safe through the wilderness.
With joy they shouted in triumph,
and walked in the light of your countenance.
You were their glory and strength,
their heads lifted high by your favour.

Refrain: The promises of God stand for ever:
when will we see them fulfilled?

You made a covenant with David your servant,
you gave him a promise to be with him for ever,
to establish his house and his throne,
to build it up for all generations.
You chose a mere youth, no warrior,
the youngest of brothers, not the eldest.
You promised to scatter his enemies,
to enlarge the bounds of his kingdom.
He called to you as his father,
his God, and the rock of his salvation.
You made him your firstborn son,
highest among the rulers of earth.

When he wandered away from your path,
when his children forsook your law,
you punished their rebellion,
you gave strength to their enemies.
And yet you betrayed not your faithfulness,
you did not profane your covenant.
Once and for all you swore by your holiness,
that you would not prove false to David.

Yet it seemed as if the promise lay shattered;
in your wrath you rejected your anointed.
You spurned the covenant with your servant,
you defiled his crown to the dust.
You broke down the walls of the city,
you made his strongholds desolate.
The scavengers swooped down to plunder,
the king was scorned by his neighbours.
You exalted the power of his enemies,
and gladdened their mocking hearts.
His bright sword lay tarnished and broken,
no longer shall he stand in the battle.
You brought his glory to an end,
you have cast down his throne to the ground.

For centuries the seed of the promise was buried,
unnoticed in the sands of the desert.
Yet human hearts cherished the hope,
waiting and yearning through oppression and exile.
At last you spoke to the young and the humble,
Mary responded to the grace of your Word.
The carpenter Joseph accepted the dream,
and the promise to David burst into life.

Your Spirit seized the being of Jesus,
anointing him in grace and in power.
The poor heard the news of acceptance and love,
the bolts of the prisoners slid back.
The blind recovered their sight,
the wounds of the victims were healed.
But the challenge of the promise was too great:
they draw back from love's fierce demands.
The incarnate of God was left quite alone,
the promise broken on the wood of the cross.

From the ashes of despair a phoenix arose,
from death's very tombs is the promise fulfilled.
The women who went to care for a corpse
were surprised with terror and joy.
Your Spirit, risen Christ, leaped through the land,
the flame that gives warmth and light to our hearts.

They expected soon your return,
that the day of your glory would dawn.
Yet again did their hopes fade away,
and the centuries began to roll by.
The promise was obscured by worldly success,
the corruptions of power, the slither of compromise.
The sufferings of children still cry aloud,
terror and greed freeze the heart still.

*O God of the Promise, but fleetingly fulfilled among us, test us not beyond
our endurance, keep hope alive, renew in us the Spirit of the risen Christ,
nourish among us the firstfruits of your harvest, and hasten the day when we
shall know the Promise has been kept.*

TIME AND ETERNITY

Refrain: Admist the confusions of time,
may we hear eternity's heartbeat.

God of eternity,
God beyond time,
our refuge and hope
from one generation to another:
Before the mountains rose from the sea,
before the rivers carved the valleys,
before time itself began,
you are God, eternal.

From dust we came,
to dust we return.
"Be shaped from the clay,
be crumbled to earth."
Creator of life, of death,
so did you order our ways.
A thousand years in your sight
are as yesterday.
As a watch in the night
comes quickly to an end,
so the years pass before you,
in a flicker of the eye.

The years are like the grass,
which in the morning is green,
and by evening is dried up and withered.
As the grass shrivels in the smoke,
so is our pride consumed in your fire:
we are afraid of the burning of the dross.

All our misdeeds and deceits
are brought to light before your eyes,
all our secret sins
made clear in the light of your truth.
When you are angry,
our days are as nothing:
our years come to an end,
vanishing with a sigh.

The decades soon pass,
no more than a handful.
Some show vigour in age,
yet even they are soon gone.
So much of our span is wearisome,
full of labour and sorrow.

O the speed of it all,
and the vanity of the years:
all I have done is like straw,
and most of it forgotten already.
Success crumbles into dust:
there is nothing to pay love's account.

Who is even aware
of the purging of your wrath?
Who pays a moment's attention
to the fierceness of your love?
Teach us to number our days,
and apply our hearts to wisdom.

Turn again, O God, do not delay:
give grace to your servants.
Satisfy us in the morning
with your lovingkindness.
So we shall rejoice and be glad
all the days of our life.

Give us days of gladness
to make up for those of affliction,
for the years of adversity.
Show your servants your deeds,
and your glory to our children.
May your grace be upon us:
fill us with the Spirit of love.
For in the evening of our days
when we come to be judged,
we shall be known only by love,
delivered only by love.

Eternal God, thank you for your gift of time and the measure death gives to our days. They pass so quickly as to dent our pride. May we neither rely on our achievements nor be downcast at our failures. Keep us but faithful to your love, and dependent on your grace alone. We ask this in the Spirit of the One who died a human failure, and died so young.

UNSHAKEABLE TRUST IN GOD

Refrain: You are trustworthy and true, my God,
holding fast to your covenant of love.

At nightfall I come to an inn on my journey,
a place of refuge, of your presence, O God,
a sanctuary, a temple, the tent of your dwelling,
where I lie down to sleep in safety.
Under the shade of your hovering wings
I have no fear of the unknown in the dark.

You have set me free from the snare of the hunter,
from the depths of the pit of snakes.
My trust in you keeps me from terror,
they sense no need to attack me.
You overshadow me with your wings,
I am safe under your feathers.
As a mother protects her brood,
so are you tender and strong towards me.
With your faithfulness as shield and defence,
I have courage to face any danger.

In the dead of night I have no terror to fear,
neither dread in the daytime the plunge of the dagger,
nor fear the plague that stalks in the darkness,
nor the fever that strikes in the heat of the day.
Though a thousand fall beside me in battle,
ten thousand at my right hand,
even though faith has endured to the limit,
still do I reach to the God who saves.

Yes, with a faith that moves mountains
still do I trust in my God.
I shall never know lasting harm,
whatever the testing ordeal.
With my own eyes I shall see
your judgment and mercy, O God.

Refrain: You are trustworthy and true, my God,
holding fast to your covenant of love.

Because I have said,
"O God, you are my hope:
you are my refuge and stronghold,"
no great evil will overwhelm me,
no final destruction crush me.
For you will command your angels
to keep me in your narrow ways:
they will bear me up in their hands
lest I dash my foot against a stone.
I may step upon cobra and adder,
but even the snakes I shall tread underfoot.
In the strength of my God,
in impossible faith,
I will bind the powers that rebel.

"Because I am bound to you in love,
therefore I will deliver you.
I will lift you out of danger
because you hold on to my name.
You know me in intimate trust,
in your inner heart you are loyal and true.
In your anguish and need I am with you,
I will set you free and clothe you with glory.
You will live to be full of years,
you will know the abundance of my salvation."

Open our eyes, O God of marvellous wonder, beyond the puzzling reflections
in the mirror, beyond the brutal images of violence, beyond the fading of the
years, that we may see the wide open spaces of promised freedom, may
glimpse the communion of saints and brush the wings of angels, may
recognize for a moment the glory of the universe, where darkness and doubt
dissolve, where the gash of the wound shines, where death and destruction
have vanished for ever.

THE STEADINESS OF GOD

Refrain: Steady and sure is the pulse of your heart,
quietening all our distress.

How precious a thing it is
to give thanks to you, O God.
How good and beautiful
to sing your name, most beloved,
to receive your love in our hearts
at the rising of the sun in the morning,
to sing of your faithfulness
in the watches of the night,
on the strings of the harp and the lyre.

In everything you have done you make me glad,
I sing for joy at the beauty of creation.
The depths of your thoughts I cannot comprehend,
the wonder of the universe I shall never fathom.
Everything that happens impinges on your heart,
in wisdom and love you hold us and heal us.
The wounds of the broken-hearted you bind,
you patiently stitch the severed limbs of your body.

The brutal do not understand your ways,
the cruel add to the pain that you suffer.
Because of the freedom you give us,
wickedness can sprout like the grass in the spring.
But in the drought of summer those who do evil
in their need have no one to turn to.
Cut off from the flow of companionship
they wither, decay, and die.
The fruits of their wrongdoing shrivel,
burnt up in the heat of your fire.

Refrain: Steady and sure is the pulse of your heart,
        quietening all our distress.

Those who have rebelled against you
will scatter their arms as they flee.
Lost and bewildered they will cower in fear,
at the mercy of those they betrayed,
whose eyes now look down on their enemies,
whose ears hear the crash of their fall.

Yet the oppressed draw near in compassion,
with water to slake their enemies' thirst.
Their deeds are as perfume so fragrant,
a precious oil with which you anoint them.
With their quiet and dignified presence
they will shame their enemies to silence.
Vibrant with life, they will invite them to dance,
their eyes glistening with laughter and joy.

Those who keep faith will flourish like the palm tree,
like the spreading cedar of Lebanon.
Planted firm in the earth of your courtyard, O God,
they will mature and give fruit for your house.
To old age they will be vigorous and fresh,
sturdy and laden with branches.
Like the trees and the mountains strong,
they will confirm your patient endurance.

God of infinite pains and patience, in these our turbulent days take from us
the stress of seeking for security in force of arms and luxury of comfort, and
give us the quiet confidence of those who have enough for today and who trust
you for tomorrow.

A CALM AUTHORITY

Refrain: To the chaos that storms, without and within,
speak with assurance, Peace, be still.

In the silence of the night your word was spoken,
a calm creative word in the heavens.
It was but a whisper of your voice,
the faint rustling of your robes of glory.
Sovereign of the universe, yet did you hide yourself,
so that your light might not shrivel us.

In quiet ways you hold the world together,
chaos contained by your compassionate power.
When the seas hurl their pounding waves,
when the hurricane howls across the ocean.
when the tornado rips through the farmland,
when the rivers rage through city streets,
still do you set a limit to their power,
that they may not overwhelm us for ever.

The surges of chaos pound through our heads,
a murderous fury rises within us;
wrenched apart by the sobbing of grief,
we are lost and bewildered, tossed to and fro.
A relentless pain throbs through our bones,
we scream in the night at the faces of terror.
Yet even as we plunge in the fearful abyss,
the face of the crucified is there in the void.

For where do we best see your power?
Nowhere else but a man who is stricken,
deserted and betrayed by his friends,
killed by his people, an outcast, unclean.
The chaos they dared not face in themselves
they hurled with abuse and the nails.
They hid from their pain in the thicket of laws,
and refused to allow their wounds to be healed.
They defended themselves in self-righteous armour,
and refused the calm word of forgiveness and love.

*Refrain: To the chaos that storms, without and within,
speak with assurance, Peace, be still.*

The material world looked so solid around us,
we never even dreamed of the chaos in matter.
As the cloud mushroomed high in the desert,
we were stunned by the force we'd unleashed.
The power of apocalypse is now in our hands:
is the calm word of God lost for ever?

*Creator God, you have entered the very fabric of the universe, for ever
committed to bringing harmony out of chaos. Assure us of your presence in
the midst of our perplexities and fears, that you will endure with us and
speak the calm word of a deeper and more lasting peace.*

THAT JUSTICE BE DONE

Refrain: Hungry for mercy,
thirsty for justice,
fierce is our cry:
Put right what is wrong.

A child is murdered in the street,
a widow is mugged for a meagre purse,
a stone shatters the bedroom window
of a couple whose skin is strange.
A violent spirit runs amok,
and the powerless are the first to suffer.

Masked gunman, why do you kill?
Arrogant fool, why do you trample?
Drunken gang, why have your hearts
become the very stones that you throw?
What is this rampaging spirit
that sweeps the mob to such fury?

No wonder the widower weeps,
no wonder the mother howls.
No wonder they shrink back in fear
or cry, Revenge, through broken glass.
O God, stop these horrors of our every day,
this wasteland of our killing fields.

How long will the ways of violence triumph?
How long will cruel words pierce the air?
How long will the arrogant boast of their conquests?
How long will prejudice keep us apart?
O God, do you not hear, do you not see?
Will you not chasten? Where is your justice?

Arise, Judge of all the earth.
May your justice be seen to be done.
Lift the burdens of oppression,
heal the crushed in mind and spirit,
bind up the wounds of the injured,
bend the necks that are stiffened with pride.

Refrain: Hungry for mercy,
thirsty for justice,
fierce is our cry: .
Put right what is wrong.

You know the thoughts of all our hearts,
you know that each of us is no more than a breath.
Yet you will not cast us away, people of the earth,
you will not forsake those you have created.
Justice will be seen to flourish again,
vindicating those who are true of heart.

Take up the cause of the weak and helpless,
speak for those overpowered by words,
bring to light the corruptions of justice,
bind those who spread evil by means of the law,
expose the conspiracies of silence,
let not the innocent be condemned.

If you had not been our helper,
we should have lost our way in the mists.
When our feet slipped on the narrow path
you held us firm in your merciful strength.
In all the anxieties of our minds
your peace steadied and calmed us.
In all the doubtings of our hearts
your presence sustained and consoled us.

Humble those who work evil,
silence those whose words weave corruption.
Gently withdraw the sting of their violence:
with healing ointment may their poison dissolve.
Remove the power of those who wreak havoc,
put them to tasks of service and care.

In your good time bring us face to face,
oppressors and victims who often collude.
None of us has words of defence in your presence,
we are silenced by the power of your truth and your love.
May the victims among us stretch out our hands
to touch those who would now shrink away,
gently to turn their faces towards us,
that our eyes may fill with mercy and wonder.

So may we look with confidence towards you,
loving God, so awesome in mercy,
fierce in compassion and judgment,
yearning for reconciliation and peace,
bearing the pain with a heartfelt cry,
in which grief and joy become one.

*Spirit of the living God, in communion with you and with the cries of those
who suffer injustice, work in and through us new deeds of discerning
wisdom and true judgment, that we may know among us the fulfilment of
your promises, even the firstfruits of your reign of justice.*

ENCOUNTERING THE REDEEMING CREATOR

Refrain: Let us sing to the One who is creating us,
let us renew our covenant with God.

Let us sing to the God who is creating us,
let us rejoice in the Rock of of our salvation.

Dear God, we celebrate your presence with thanksgiving,
and with our whole heart sing psalms of praise.
We greet you with love, Creator of the universe,
Spirit who strives with the chaos of the world.
With your finger you shape the mountains of the earth,
and the depths of the valleys are scoured by your power.
The wings of your Spirit brood over the seas,
and your hands mould the dry land.

Not one of the threatening powers escapes you,
the thundering of the gods on the cloud-capped mountains,
the rumbling of demons as the earth quakes,
the faces that loom in the dreams of the night,
the punishing voices from our helpless past.
The power of your love reaches so far
that nothing and no-one is beyond your redemption.

O come let us worship and lift our hearts high
and adore our God, our Creator.
For you indeed are God, and we are your people,
crafted by the skill of your hands.

"Listen to my voice this day
and harden not your hearts.
Do not be like your ancestors
who saw the great deeds I had done,
yet put me to the test in the desert,
at the place of Bitterness and Quarrel.

"They were wayward in their hearts,
they were ignorant of my ways.
So they could sense but the wrath of my love,
and were condemned to a restless wandering."

If we listen to your voice deep within us,
we shall know the mercy and grace of your love.
We shall see you as Judge of the earth,
doing right in the sight of all peoples,
judging us all in your faithfulness,
quelling our rebellious strife.

Spirit of Christ, take shape among us,
Spirit of the One who fulfilled God's promise.
Humble us in awe at your presence:
let us adore you in the silence of love.
Deepen our gratitude in obedience and trust,
in your covenant made sure for ever.

To the beauty and bounty of your creation and grace, we have responded, O God, with desecration and greed. We have presumed upon the constant renewal of your gifts. Give us penitent hearts and the will to cherish the earth, that we may know you again as our redeeming Creator, bringing good from our wastes and sorrows.

JOY IN GOD

Refrain: Sing to the great God a new song,
sing to the Creator, sing the whole earth.
Let nature and peoples join in harmony
to sing praise to the God of glory.

We sing to you, God, and praise your name,
telling of your salvation from day to day,
declaring your glory to those who do not know you,
and your wonders to the peoples of the earth.
Marvellous God, you are greatly to be praised,
more to be honoured than all the powers.
Glory and worship are before you,
power and honour are in your sanctuary.

May we, the household of your people,
ascribe to you worship and glory,
giving you the honour due to your name,
bringing presents as we come into your house.
We worship you in the beauty of holiness:
let the whole earth stand in awe of you.
Let us tell it out among the peoples that you are God,
and that you are making the round world so sure,
held within the bounds of your love,
and that you will judge the people righteously.

Let the heavens rejoice and let the earth be glad:
let the sea roar, and all its creatures delight;
let the fields be joyful, and all that is in them:
then shall the trees of the wood shout for joy.
For you come to judge the earth,
with justice to make right what is wrong,
to judge the people with your truth.

All creatures of the earth will sing your praise,
for you are a God who is faithful,
for ever loyal to your covenant,
creating out of discord a harmony rare.

God of glory and splendour, whose bright radiance we see in glimpses of wonder, both rare and everyday, open our eyes and hearts, alert the nerve ends of our being, that in trembling and rapture all our fears may dissolve into joy.

THE OLD ORDER TURNED UPSIDE DOWN

Refrain: God reigns: the gentle people inherit the earth,
the little islands rejoice to see the day.

The foundations of your reign are rarely seen, O God,
salvation and justice are hidden away.
Clouds and darkness deepen the mystery:
faith hears but a possible cry.

The God of Justice comes:
the thunder rolls,
the lightnings flash,
the earth quakes.
Evil is burnt up by fire,
the mountains melt like wax;
the flames consume corruption,
the falling rocks hiss in the sea.

We have served vain idols,
and we are ashamed,
awed by the searing truth,
in fear and trembling brought to our knees.
Your glory lights up our faces,
and our eyes are blinded.
We have put lovers and leaders before you,
we have bowed down to our petty gods,
we have gloried in mere nothings:
like them we crumble to the dust.

The City of Peace hears its God,
and all its inhabitants rejoice.
In your judgment, O God, are the poor lifted high,
the burdens of oppression slide from their backs.
For you love those who resist evil,
you guard the life of the faithful,
you sustain them when held in the grip
of the cruel and greedy and hateful.

Your promised day dawns, O God,
a day of gladness for the true of heart.
Your reign spreads fair before us,
like a banquet prepared for a homecoming.
Those who love truth flourish in your presence,
their faces glow in the light of your welcome.
The courageous and faithful sing for joy,
and give thanks to your glorious name.

In the day of your vindication, O God, we shall laugh and sing as we never
have before. From our bellies will flow the ripples of joy, the living water
that makes the desert bloom and the true of heart delight in one another's love.

THE SONG OF A RENEWED CREATION

Refrain: Praise to the God who makes all things new;
let all creation sing a new song.

We praise you, O God, with a new song,
for you have done marvellous things.
With your own right hand and with your holy arm,
with the strength of weakness and the endurance of waiting,
you have achieved the greatest of victories,
bringing triumph from the midst of defeat.

So you have declared your salvation,
showing justice in the sight of the peoples.
You have remembered your mercy and faithfulness
towards the house of Israel;
your salvation has shone forth
even to the far-flung islands of the world.

Show yourselves joyful in God, all you peoples,
sing, rejoice, and give thanks.
We praise you, O God, upon the harp,
singing a psalm of thanksgiving,
with trumpets and echoing horns,
showing ourselves joyful in your presence.

Let the sea roar, and all its creatures,
the round earth, and those who dwell on it.
Let the streams clap their hands,
and let the hills be joyful before you.

For you have come to judge the earth,
justified at last in your sight,
and judging the people with justice,
with a mercy beyond our comparing,
O holy, compassionate, and most loving God.

Faithful Creator, ever striving with your creation, with nature, with your
people, with the One who embodied your will, bringing new and unexpected
life out of despair and death, work still in these our days, that we may sing
a new song to your glory.

HOLY IS GOD

Refrain: Holy, holy, holy is the living God,
holy in the awesome intimacy of love,
holy in the terrible demands of love,
holy in the silent suffering of love.

Holy God, you reign throughout the universe,
enthroned as a king majestic and just,
kneeling before us as a healer with wounds,
touching our foreheads as a woman who is wise.
Creatures of light and darkness surround you,
eyes glistening with tears of thanksgiving.

Yours is the power that holds,
the power of justice and love.
Yours is the holiness that sears,
bringing to light our falsehoods.
The prophets, the priests, and the wise,
Moses and Aaron, Samuel and Solomon,
call assured upon your name,
knowing that you will teach them,
showing them how to lead the people,
burning into them your holiness,
never yielding the commandment to love,
refusing to let any of us sink deep
into the mire and oblivion of sin.

Holy was your presence in the love of your Christ,
always in places the pious rejected,
born in a cave among a people oppressed,
suffering the hidden cost of forgiveness,
embracing the outcast who were deemed impure,
dying disgraced and disfigured,
even on a cross that was holy and hopeful.

Holy God, teach us not to be afraid of anything or anyone you have created,
however threatened or repelled we may be. Fill us with your Holy Spirit, the
holiness that draws near to transform, the Spirit that finds its home, as you
did, in our flesh and blood.

A JOYFUL PEOPLE

Refrain: We joy in your steadfast love,
we rejoice and are thankful.

Let the whole earth be joyful in you, O God,
serve you with gladness,
and celebrate your presence with a song.

For we know that you are creating us,
you have made us and we belong to you,
We are your people, and the sheep of your pasture.

We find our way into your gates with thanksgiving,
and into your house with praise.
We give you thanks and bless your holy name.

For you are gracious, your mercy is everlasting,
and your faithfulness endures from generation to generation.

Living, loving, holy God, our joy rests in you and comes from you, for we
are indeed content to be your people and we are humbled by your care for us.
You are God and there is none other. You are steadfast, faithful, loyal, and
kind. We would seek to embody your will on earth, and to trust you for all
that is to come.

PSALMS 101–150

THE SINGLE EYE

Refrain: Pierce our hearts with the light of your love,
our minds with the sword of your truth.

Take from us, O God, the burden of pretence,
the lie that we and our leaders are just.
Let songs of wisdom sound from our lips;
keep self-righteousness far from our hearts.

So often we pretend to be innocent,
blameless and free of all guilt.
Open our eyes that we may see clear:
there is no escaping our crookedness.

So often we slander our neighbours,
afraid of their class or colour or creed.
Expose to the light the projections of our minds:
it is ourselves we should see in their mirror.

So often we are angry with the greedy and proud,
the arrogant who are deaf to the cries of the poor.
Keep our eye single; give us hearts that are pure,
lest we trample without knowing what we do.

So often we grumble at people with power,
calling them deceitful and corrupt in their ways.
Humble us all whose eyes are so blurred:
dishonest we are, we discern not the truth.

So often we fail to take account of our wealth,
the power of body, possessions, or talent.
May the light that shines from the eyes of the humble
burn out the corruption to which we are blind.

God of truth, hold before our eyes a vision of your commonwealth, your reign
of integrity and wisdom, justice and mercy. Give to those in public life
minds that are true and hearts that are compassionate. May they be humbled
by those who pass by.

RESURRECTION PROMISE

Refrain: *To the One who has disappeared,*
to the Presence we know as Absence,
we wave with the shreds of our faith,
Is the power of death overturned?

We live through a night of deep trouble,
of dreams that disturb, of collapse and decay.
We restore the façades of our heritage,
but within the meaning has gone.
Even the stones turn to dust,
as the beauty of the ages departs.
The lines of power strut the landscape:
the energy that feeds them fails.

The smoke of my days rises in the twilight,
curls in the air and is gone.
Already my bones blaze in the furnace,
reduced to the ash that soon they shall be.
My heart is scorched and shrivels,
pounded like grass in the summer heat.
The groans of my throat shrink to a croak,
my skin is glued to my bones.

Like a bird that is trapped by midwinter,
I find no food in the frozen waste.
Anxiously I look all around me,
afraid of the swoop of my enemies.
Chattering and restless I flit to and fro,
screeching through the desolate silence.
Exhausted, I limp through the snow;
I sink to the earth, shot through by the wind.

Slowly, steadily, I turn to you, my hope,
daring still to whisper your name.
Surely your heart moves with pity,
even to the grey streaks of my hair?

Your name has been known by my ancestors,
my children will seek and will find.
The nations will at last sing your praise,
the rulers of the peoples give you glory.

Your heart must surely hear the cry of the destitute,
you cannot despise your little ones.
The wounded you embrace with compassion,
you slide back the bolts of the prisoners.
Oh, it sounds so glib – though we say it in faith –
so nearly like vain repetition.
We desperately want to believe it is true,
that those yet unborn may give you the praise.

You have broken my strength before my time,
the very days cut short, their gift snatched away.
Soon I shall perish, and yet you endure,
my clothes become rags, yet your years never fail.
A comfort perhaps – but the children still die,
and the barren know nothing but dust.
Can the young Man who died give us hope?
The cry of the night be answered with joy?

Where is the language of words that catch fire?
Where is the wonder of a birth that is new?
Where is the savour of salt on the breeze?
Where is the bouquet of the freshest of wines?
Where is the confounding of the powers in the land?
Where is the community indifferent to threat?
Where are the alert, the wise and compassionate?
Where are the gifts whose giving does not end?

*Your promises, O God, stand for ever, yet our hearts are torn when we see
them unfulfilled, even the crumbs of reassurance fail to fall, and we are
shrivelled by perplexity and doubt. Keep us faithful through our winter.
May the slender thread hold.*

UNFATHOMABLE LOVE

Refrain: There is no end to your mercy,
enduring and infinite is your love.

From the deep places of my soul I praise you, O God:
I lift up my heart and glorify your holy name.
From the deep places of my soul I praise you, O God:
how can I forget all your goodness towards me?

You forgive all my sin, you heal all my weakness,
you rescue me from the brink of disaster,
you crown me with mercy and compassion.
You satisfy my being with good things,
so that my youth is renewed like an eagle's.

You fulfil all that you promise,
justice for all the oppressed.
You made known your ways to Moses,
and all the people saw your deeds.

You are full of forgiveness and grace,
endlessly patient, faithful in love.
You do not haunt us with our sins,
nor nurse grievances against us.
You do not repay evil with evil,
for you are greater than our sins.

As vast as the heavens are in comparison with the earth,
so great is your love to those who trust you.
As far as the east is from the west,
so far do you fling our sins from us.

Just as parents are merciful to their children,
so are you merciful and kind towards us.
For you know how fragile we are,
that we are made of the dust of the earth.
Our days are like the grass,
they bloom like the flowers of the field:
the wind blows over them and they are gone,
and no-one can tell where they stood.

Only your merciful goodness endures;
age after age you act justly
towards all who hold on to your covenant,
who take your words to heart and fulfil them.

For you have triumphed over the power of death,
and draw us to your presence with songs of joy.
We hear the echo of your angels praising you,
and the whole communion of your saints,
those who have walked in your narrow ways,
and heard the voice of your yearning,
whose food is to do your will,
and in whom you take great delight.

From the widest bounds of the universe
to the depths of my very being
the whispers and cries of joy
vibrate to a shining glory,
O God, our beginning and our end.

Creator God, as we contemplate the vast universe of which we are so small a part, swamping us with fear and despair and our insignificance, deepen our trust that the profoundest meaning of it all is Love, beyond whose reach it is impossible to fall.

EXUBERANT WONDER

Refrain: *Marvellous and vigorous,*
splendidly unfolding,
the wonders of creation
we contemplate with awe.

Praise be to the Creator:
fresh energy divine,
with passion and with tenderness,
brings beauty new to birth.

Light from the dawn of the cosmos,
reaching out over billions of years;
the sun so familiar and steady,
spun off from that ancient fireball:
the primal explosion murmurs,
we hear the hiss of the aeons,
whispering insistent relic
of the original moment of time.
The beginning was all flame,
and the flame was unfurled into time;
all that has come into being
began at the heart of the flame.
Slowly the fire cooled,
the storm of particles ceased,
combed into structures of matter,
clouds and clusters of galaxies.
The cosmic dust was scattered –
a heart bursting into stars:
truly strange is our ancestor –
we ride on its pulsing still.   *Refrain*

Alone we seem in the darkness,
puppets of impersonal forces,
at best a mere flicker of light,
extinguished against the night sky.

But look at the world of the atom,
a minute yet infinite space,
where the unpredictable happens,
place of the improbably new.
Innumerable fragments that scattered
our consciousness begins to make whole,
mysteriously linked to our minds,
synapses by the billion in our brains.
Sounds stir through our bodies,
themselves fashioned by the stars,
bound up with the smallest particles.
Each of us seems like a universe.
Do we see deep in your mind,
more incredible still, our Creator?
To and fro have you ceaselessly woven
this web of matter and energy? *Refrain*

We stand on a cliff top and watch,
gazing out over infinite seas,
whence our ancestors lately emerged,
obeying the call to a more complex life.
And still in the teeming oceans
swim the marvellous creatures,
the vital plankton sustaining them,
on which we also depend.
There go the whales and the dolphins,
even, it is rumoured, Leviathan,
that great monster of the deep,
the delight and sport of our God.
The heat of the sun draws the moisture
up from the seas to the turbulent skies,
where the winds blow the rain-bearing clouds
to fall on the mountains and valleys.
Thence spring the rivers and streams,
watering the brown of the earth into green,
quenching the thirst of the animals,
bearing the people in trade and in play. *Refrain*

Refrain: Marvellous and vigorous,
            splendidly unfolding,
            the wonders of creation
            we contemplate with awe.

Praise be to the Creator:
fresh energy divine,
with passion and with tenderness,
brings beauty new to birth.

The eyes of the satellites roam,
the soaring balloons hover,
the gliders smoothly range,
they see the mosaics of earth.
There in the tangle of rain forests
is the clicking of insects, the slither of snakes,
the screech of parrots, the blanket of rain,
and numberless species yet to be named.
There jostle the shining mountains,
lands of the long white clouds,
eagles soaring to their eyries,
snow leopards ruling the heights.
There ripple the sands of the desert,
where the barren flowers at the touch of rain,
where the fennec fox watches and listens,
through the deep silence that falls with the night.
The lions of the savannahs roar,
the cedars of Lebanon spread their branches,
the cattle graze in the pastures,
the cats curl up in the sun.   *Refrain*

We harvest the goodness of earth,
we reap the wheat and the maize,
we pluck the grapes from the vine,
the olives from the gnarled branches.
You give us an abundance to share,
the loaves of life for the table,
wine to gladden our hearts,
oil to lighten our skin.

Yet the sun can scorch the corn,
the lava snap the trees,
the hurricane flatten the houses,
the tidal waves and river floods drown.
The meteors hurtle through space,
the stars explode and vanish,
the violence our hearts abhor,
yet playing its vital part.
We may believe your Spirit created
and renews the face of the earth:
the destruction tempers our praise,
darkened by pain and perplexity.   *Refrain*

*Creator God, we celebrate a new unfolding of the universe this day, in us
and in everything around us. We listen to the silence and we hear the rustling
of our breath, the hum of engines, the cries of birds . . . We question and we
adore . . . we wonder . . . we trust . . .*

THE COVENANTS OF GOD

Refrain: Give praise to the God of the Promise,
who keeps faith with the earth for ever.

Let us give thanks to you, O God, and call upon your name;
let us tell among the peoples the things you have done.
We sing to you, we sing your praise,
and tell of all your marvellous works.
We exult in your holy name;
even in our seeking we are joyful in heart.
Let us seek your wisdom and strength,
let us seek the compassion of your face.
Let us call to mind the wonders you have done,
your marvellous acts and your discerning judgments. *Refrain*

Time was when we were but a few,
small in number and aliens in the land.
We wandered from valley to valley,
from one oasis and people to another.
Even then you protected us,
keeping at bay those who would harm us.
Then you called down a famine on the land,
and destroyed the bread that we needed.
But you sent on a man ahead of us,
Joseph who was sold into slavery,
whose feet the Egyptians fastened with fetters,
and thrust his neck into a hoop of iron.
He was tested to the limit by his captors,
until the time when his words proved true.
Then the pharaoh sent word to release him,
to become steward of all his household,
to order his officers at will,
and to teach his counsellors wisdom.   *Refrain*

Then Israel came into Egypt,
and Jacob dwelt in the land of Ham.
There you made your people fruitful,
too numerous for those who opposed us,
whose hearts you turned to hate us
and deal deceitfully with your servants.
Then you sent Moses your servant,
and Aaron whom you had chosen.
Through them you worked your signs,
and your wonders in the land of Ham.
You sent darkness to cover the land,
the darkness of your ways that we do not understand.
You turned their waters into blood,
and the fish rose dead to the surface.
Their country swarmed with frogs,
even into the house of the pharaoh.
You spoke the word and there came swarms of flies,
and gnats within all their borders.
You sent them storms of hail,
and darts of lightning into their land.
You struck their vines and their fig trees,
you sent locusts to devour their crops.
Death and decay spread its misery,
even to the firstborn of each family.   *Refrain*

You brought Israel out with silver and gold,
and not one of our tribes was seen to stumble.
Egypt was glad at our going,
for dread of Israel had fallen upon them.
You spread out a cloud for our covering,
and fire to lighten the night.
The people asked and you brought us quails,
and satisfied us with manna from your hand.
You opened a rock so that the waters gushed,
and ran in the parched land like a river,
For you had remembered your holy word,
the promise to Abraham your servant.
So you led out your people with rejoicing,
your chosen ones with shouts of joy.

Refrain: Give praise to the God of the promise,
who keeps faith with the earth for ever.

You gave us the land you had promised,
and we inherited the toil of others,
so that we might keep the gift of your law,
and faithfully fulfil your covenant.   *Refrain*

So we remember our ancestors' story,
how they knew you as the God of the promise.
Out of your limitless love
you have chosen, O God, to be bound
with the limits of body and time
to the earth and all its people.
For you renew the covenants of old,
ever deepening your promise to love.
In the covenant of exodus from Egypt
you brought the people out of slavery.
In the covenant of Sinai with Moses
you gave shape and meaning to their lives.
In the covenant with Abraham and Isaac,
with Jacob and their descendants for ever,
you vowed your loyalty to them,
giving them the land of the promise,
and requiring the response of their hearts,
a steady will to trust and obey.   *Refrain*

You sustain your covenant with Noah,
with the living creatures of earth,
that never again will you destroy them,
with a flood laying waste to the world.
Your love is for the whole of our planet,
a vow of restraint and protection for ever.
Again and again you renew your promise,
putting a new heart and spirit within us,
through a covenant sealed by your blood,
your last will and testament for us.   *Refrain*

You demand no unthinking obedience,
a loyalty blind and correct.
You do not try to control us,
you seek the pledge of our wills and our hearts.
You are the One who endures our betrayals,
with a precarious and vulnerable love.
You keep faith with us and humble us,
and so renew us in hope.
You laid down the power of coercion,
and gave of yourself with generous love.
Our hearts burst out with gratitude,
in awe at the wonder of your goodness.
You have bound yourself to us – we belong to you,
and to one another – there is no way to escape.
Keep us responding in friendship and service,
giving and receiving your presence among us,
protecting those who are weak and in need,
trust deepening in sacraments of love.　　　　*Refrain*

*In the mystery of Divine Love, we become gifts to one another, bound
together in the covenants of God. In the paradox of our free will and destiny
let us all embrace, choosing in friendship to share our being and becoming.
And with that divine love, and in the spirit of that love, let us promise to be
steady and reliable in our loving for ever, to work for our mutual well-being
and the cherishing of our earth, to honour one another as God's dwelling
place, and to keep loyal and full of faith, our life-day long.*

AS OUR ANCESTORS DID

Refrain: Open our eyes that we may see
the harm we have done in the world.
Open our ears that we may hear
your word of warning and mercy.
Draw us through the narrowest of gates
to the wide open space of the promise.

O God of our ancestors we praise you
for your goodness and mercy for ever.
We can but stammer our gratitude,
so marvellous and mysterious are your ways.
Only the just and humble of heart
can sound the depths of the story.
In remembering the times that are past,
renew us in penitence and hope.
Come alive in us with the power that heals
that we may share in your freedom and love.
Let your shalom spread over the land:
let us rejoice that we belong to you for ever.   *Refrain*

We disobey you as our ancestors did:
we act perversely and do what is wrong.
We are glad in our moments of freedom,
whenever you deliver us from Egypt.
But soon we forget the wealth of your love,
filled with fear of those who pursue us.
You clear our way through the quaking marsh,
parting the reeds for the fleet of foot.
Heavy with chariots our enemies sink,
and no one returns with their story.
Bowed down by oppressions of self and of others
we cry out for help and you throw off our burdens.
Light of step we go on our way,
rejoicing in your love and singing your praise.   *Refrain*

It takes but a moment to forget you,
we blunder along and wait not for your counsel.
We cannot face how empty we are,
and greed takes hold in the desert.
In our craving we put you to the test,
and you give what we say we desire.
But envy and bitterness seize us,
and the loathing we have for ourselves
we project on to those who are holy,
like Moses and Aaron of old.
Faction and quarrel spread unchecked,
we are secretly glad when our neighbours fall.
"Let the earth itself swallow them up;
let fire burn our rivals even as they sleep."   *Refrain*

Many are the idols we have made as our gods,
golden calves of comfort and money.
Again and again we exchange your glory
for the pursuit of the utterly worthless.
So easily do we forget what you have done
to bring us out of enslavement.
We need the holy ones we scapegoat
who can bear the fierceness of your love,
the fiery anger that would consume us,
did Moses not stand in the breach.   *Refrain*

We refuse to recognize the gifts that you give,
our faith in your promise evaporates.
We grumble and murmur in our tents
and refuse to listen to your voice.
You lift up your hand against us,
to scatter us through the wilderness,
our children losing their respect,
and vanishing far and wide.
We turn to the many false comforters,
wanting change without cost to ourselves.
Still do we eat the food of the dead,
though it is but ashes in our mouths.
We provoke you to anger by our foolishness,
and the body starts breaking apart.

Refrain: Open our eyes that we may see
the harm we have done in the world.
Open our ears that we may hear
your word of warning and mercy.
Draw us through the narrowest of gates
to the wide open space of the promise.

Plagues rage round the world,
and few there are with the courage
to sacrifice their own comforts and wealth,
like Phinehas to draw near to your presence,
taking to themselves the wraths and the sorrows,
standing firm as the beacons of hope.
And yes, we embitter our leaders,
who in turn become faithless and rash.
So Moses suffered for our misdeeds,
when you were angry at the waters of Meribah. *Refrain*

We did not destroy the inhabitants of the land.
Did you not command us to cleanse it?
Should we have dismissed them from our hearts,
making them less than human in our sight?
But we did not even stand up for your truths,
we sought to make ourselves acceptable to them.
We started to follow their customs,
mingling in family and marriage.
We were seduced into worshipping idols,
and snared into deeds still more cruel.
With bloodlust we butchered our children,
surrendering to the demonic within us.
So the rivers were defiled with blood;
we made ourselves foul by our deeds. *Refrain*

No wonder your anger blazed,
so obtuse and wicked had we become.
It seemed that you loathed your own people,
for you gave us to the hand of our enemy.
The rule of the oppressor stifled us,
stripping us of value and dignity.

Though you rescued us many a time,
yet we fell once again in our evil.
Nevertheless you looked on our distress,
you heard the cry of our lament.
You remembered your covenant with us,
and relented in mercy and pity.
Before the very eyes of our enemies
your love kept working to free us.
Preserve us, O God, gather us together,
that we may reverence and praise you for ever.   *Refrain*

Did you command your people to destroy,
to commit even genocide according to your will?
Were their enemies so utterly evil
that not one of them deserved to survive?
Despite the rebellion of our ancestors
you spared them and graced them still.
Is your covenant only for a few who are favoured,
flourishing at the expense of the many?
Is not the pure race a dangerous myth,
an illusion that has never been real?
Did not your people misunderstand your call
to be special for service, not privilege?
Such old rigid thoughts are too proud,
too dangerous for our fragile earth home.
Your covenant is with all that you have made,
loving all creation through pain to its glory.
Your power, not almighty in magic,
neither capricious nor blind in its force,
will sustain and redeem your world yet,
withholding your fierce scalding fire,
refining in the heat of your love,
bringing out of evil unimaginable good.   *Refrain*

*May we never become so angry that we lose touch with compassion. May
we receive divine wrath only as an aspect of divine love. May we never lose
respect for other human beings, created in the image of God. May we be
empowered by the Spirit to overcome all desire to harm and all prejudice that
treats others as less than human. O God, make us and keep us Christlike.*

THE CRY FOR RESCUE

We give you thanks, O God, for you are gracious,
and your mercy endures for ever.
You bear the awful cost of our rescue,
redeeming us from terror and pain.
Even as the relentless winds of the universe
raged through the silence of the ages,
your heart was stirring to bring us to life,
to gather as gifts to one another.

You are with us through all our bewilderments,
through the impenetrable mystery of evil and pain,
redeeming our wastes and our sorrows,
hiding from us the glory to come.

Sometimes we are strangers on the earth,
wanderers with no room to call our own.
We go astray in the wilderness,
lost in the trackless desert.
The mists come down in the mountains,
we wander on the featureless moors.
Aimlessly stumbling in the forests,
we find no way to a city to dwell in.
Hungry and thirsty, our spirits sink within us;
we languish and collapse, ready to die.

Then we cry to you, O God, in our troubles,
and you deliver us from our distress.

You set our feet on a path we had not seen,
and you lead us to a place we can make as our own.

Let us praise you, O God, for your goodness,
your lovingkindness to the children of earth.
With nourishing food you have satisfied us,
you have slaked our aching thirst.

We sit in darkness and the shadow of death,
shackled by misery and affliction.
We are signs of a world ill at ease,
broken and distressed, hearts torn apart,
tossing to and fro in rebellion,
spurning the word of our own deepest good.
Our wits are blurred by our troubles,
under their weight we stagger and fall.
Shamed by our guilt, trembling with fear,
isolated and lonely, we find no one to help.

Then we cry to you, O God, in our troubles,
and you deliver us from our distress.

You break the chains that keep us imprisoned,
you lead us gently by the hand and into the sun.

Let us praise you, O God, for your goodness,
your lovingkindness to the children of earth.
You have shattered the doors of bronze,
you have snapped in two the iron bars.

When we go down to the sea in ships
or take to the air in great birds,
we are overcome with fear and with awe
at your wonders in the deep and in the skies.
For at your word the stormy wind arises,
lifting the waves of the sea,
stirring the turbulent clouds.
We are carried up to the heavens,
and down again to the depths:
we are tossed to and fro in peril,
we reel and stagger like drunkards,
our craftsmanship is all in vain.

Then we cry to you, O God, in our troubles,
and you deliver us from our distress.

Storms without and within cease at your word,
the waves of the sea and the air are stilled.
We recover our poise, panic leaves us,
we discover a presence that guides us through.

Then we are glad because we are at rest,
and you bring us to the haven where we would be.

Let us praise you, O God, for your goodness,
your lovingkindness to the children of earth.
At the gathering of the congregation your name be praised.
From the seat of the elders may you be glorified.

Yet again we turn to our foolishness,
caught in the cycles of disease and rebellion.
We turn away from the food that nourishes us,
even though we are brought to death's door.
We are caught in traps of poverty,
unable to move, hemmed in to despair.
We are bound by the scripts of our ancestors,
their sinewy subtleties holding us fast.

Then we cry to you, O God, in our troubles—
not always do you deliver us from our distress.

Your word of release sometimes heals us,
and we know we are saved from destruction.

It is hard to do more than whisper our thanks,
we lose hold of the mystery of your goodness.
Sometimes the helplessness in which we are caught
cries out in the night with no answering word.

The perplexity of your ways gives us pain;
we live between prison and freedom.
One day are the doors flung open,
only for others to close on the next.
You turn the rivers into beds of parched stones,
you dry up the springs of water.
You make the fertile land barren,
mirroring the drought of our goodness.
You fill the desert sands with water,
in the dry ground fresh springs emerge.
You bring in those who are hungry
to settle there and till the soil.
We plough fields, plant vineyards,
reap crops, graze herds.

We are blessed and our numbers increase,
yet the very next moment we seem cursed.
One day we are well content,
the next diminished again –
with plague, famine and war,
with stress in adversity and sorrow.
Even the powerful are brought low
and wander again in the desert.
And you raise up the poor from affliction,
making them strong in the land.

Only the eye of faith can discern your ways,
and even then they mightily puzzle us.
But let us be wise and ponder these things,
wisdom still finds her way to your praise.
Ever and again you protect and restrain us,
always with yet more gifts in store.
Let us therefore praise you, O God, for your goodness,
Your lovingkindness to the children of earth.

Keep us faithful, O God, trusting in your promise and power to rescue and
redeem. In the darker places of faith's journey help us to discern our freedom
in choosing what is difficult as if it were easy. For then we shall have faith
indeed, and even at the bleakest times we shall praise.

THE MAKING OF MUSIC

Refrain: *With the voice of song*
and the sounds of nature,
with the instruments of melody
and the strains of the heart,
with the discords let loose
and the cries unshaped,
we seek to make music,
the music of God.

May the instruments of music
come alive in our hands.
May the flute and the harp
sing the praises of God.
May the strings of my heart
make melody in the morning.
May the song of my soul
be echoed by the dawn.
While oppression weighs heavy,
and grief bows the heart,
let songs of consolation
lighten the load.
Beloved, you embrace the universe,
reaching the depths of our darkness.
The music of your glory shimmers,
your faithfulness ever its theme.
The earth and all its inhabitants
you orchestrate into beauty.
For however discordant we sound,
you are always creating new harmonies.   *Refrain.*

In the music of poetry and song,
in the laughter of highland streams,
in the melody of curlew and nightingale,
we are joined in praise of your beauty,
We relish the names of the rivers,
the mountains, the lakes, and the forests,
the villages, towns, and cities,
the countries that stir our hearts.
All of them make music to you, O God,
each one of them part of your vesture,
a theme in the symphony of praise,
the sound of their name giving you glory.   *Refrain*

The trumpet calls the army to war,
the horn gives warning to the city.
The drumbeat swells our pride,
our feet tap out in unison.
"With God on our side we will conquer."
Victory is sweet music to our ears.
The armies clash, the harmonies shatter –
can the screech of the dying sing your praise?   *Refrain*

Where now is the music of hope?
A new sound from the heart of our God?
Can the trumpet and horn caress,
can the beat of the drum make us dance?
Will the way of the Christ bear fruit
from seeds of non-violent passion?
Can the discords of evil be transformed
in the searing flames of your love?
Can the powers that harm be disarmed?
Is our love strong enough to contain them?
Then we would hear such harmonies
as the world can barely imagine.
We would know our place in the making of music,
our very need for enemies banished for ever.   *Refrain*

*In the music of lament and celebration, of loyalties and questioning, of love
and protest, of ballad and cantata, we seek to be your partners, Creator God,
in the weaving of the patterns of glory. Inspire us, guide us, transform us.*

AN ANGRY AND FEARSOME CRY

Refrain: In the hope that defies despair,
when goodness itself is paralysed,
and the voices of praise fall silent,
the stones themselves cry out,
the pitying creatures put us to shame,
the earth's ancient wisdom warns.

Let us speak out for the silenced,
giving voice to the voiceless.
Let the screams be uncorked,
and the bellows of rage resound.
The cry of the abused and violated
has far too long been unheard.
The ignorance of those uninvolved
colludes with the guilty and shamed,
all conspiring in silence,
their wounds festering unseen.   *Refrain*

The wealthy with bribes and corruption,
the fearful blackmailed to silence,
the lawkeepers twisting the evidence,
the advocates skilled in deceit and delay,
the ministers who can never be wrong,
establishments protecting their own,
the bullies hiding their cowardice,
the soldiers with permission to kill,
their mentors warping their minds
to think of the enemy as vermin,
the women a target for rape:
all fall under the cursing.
For the present we withhold God's blessing,
while refraining to crush in our turn.   *Refrain*

And the women cry out in pain,
and the men and the childen too:
The blood that flows cries out for revenge –
cursed be the violence of the strong.
The child howls in the lonely night –
cursed be the hand that bruised.
The woman lies sobbing on the floor –
cursed be the hard eyes and the unyielding stone.
The body that trusted lies rigid with shock –
cursed be the relishing of pain.
The weak are intimidated and afraid –
cursed be our arrogance and lust for power.
The abused shrink away in silent shame –
cursed be the evil power of secrecy.
The abusers protest their innocence –
cursed be the refusals and denials.
The comfortable turn away, refusing to see –
cursed be our collusion and cowardice.   *Refrain*

What is the voice of the dead-strewn streets?
Of the infants buried by rubble?
"Woe to you who work evil in the land,
inventors and makers of weapons,
automatic in the spattering of blood,
of semtex packed in a purse,
exploding in the face of passers-by.
Woe to the pride of your technology,
destroyers lurking in the city's cellars,
endemic to your way of death
from the hands of desperate men.
Woe to the wars of car bombs and missiles,
the buttons and triggers of a control so remote
from the travellers blown from the skies.

Refrain: *In the hope that defies despair,*
when goodness itself is paralysed,
and the voices of praise fall silent,
the stones themselves cry out,
the pitying creatures put us to shame,
the earth's ancient wisdom warns.

Woe to the traders in arms,
woe to the traffickers in drugs,
woe to the poisoners of minds,
woe to the serial killers,
woe to the men of cold eyes,
woe to the remorseless hearts,
woe to those with no pity." *Refrain*

O Christ of angry compassion,
sweeping away the exploiters,
moved to speak out for the little ones,
drawing the sting of oppression,
lift up the crushed in spirit,
empower them to find their own voice,
to shame the violators to penitence,
to hope for the time of forgiveness,
to strengthen the rule of law,
to heap coals of fire on their heads,
the fire of love's wrath and desire
for justice and peace to be shared
in reconciliation and joy for ever. *Refrain*

Holy and just God, receive the feelings of our outraged and wounded hearts.
Console our grief, melt our fear, lift the burden of our shame. Restrain our
desire for revenge, and channel the fierce energies of our anger in the service
of justice and truth.

POWER WITH SERVICE

Refrain: To those with power give wisdom,
the spirit of true understanding.

The oracles of old exalted the king
to stand at the right hand of God.
As priest and prince he was to rule
not by descent but by God's call.
The sceptre of power was placed in his hand,
to shatter the heads of his enemies.
Through him God routed the armies,
striding across corpses strewn in the way.

A strange world to us, faded from view,
kings riding out on horseback to conquer.
The wars of our time have tarnished the glory,
the rhetoric of God but masking our pride.
Arrogance and greed are the gods that we follow,
and even the wars we name holy or just
degrade those who wage them, reminding us all
how cruel and cold the world can become.

Yet as we dig deep in these words from the past,
we see a vision of those who would lead:
they lay on themselves the robe of the priestly,
willingly weighed down by the burden of service,
sacrificing self for the good of their land,
growing in discernment and wisdom.
They bring greater good from the conflicts around them,
and they heal the wounds of the people.

God of Wisdom, guide those in power with your Spirit of true counsel, that
they may discern the course that is just, sacrificing themselves for the
common good, not only of their own country but of the whole earth, laying
aside all pride of wealth and status. And may we all find the courage to use
whatever power we have.

THE HEARTBEAT OF GOD

Refrain: The heartbeat of God, the Amen of love,
faithful for ever, steady and sure.

My gratitude, O God, flows on,
like the deep and silent river,
I join in the stream of praise,
with your people gathered for worship.
We take our place in the Story,
re-kindled in the seasons' round.
We celebrate your mercies of old,
and your deeds among us today.

The great words resound in our ears,
we delight in the God who embodies them:
your glory and splendour and justice,
your beauty and grace and compassion,
your truth and faithfulness for ever,
your covenant of promise and life,
your creative and redeeming power,
your holiness, wisdom, and love.

Day by day you nourish us,
feeding us with sacrament and word,
slaking our thirst from the wellspring,
the waters that never run dry.
You renew your covenant each morning,
loyal to your promise for ever.
Awesome is your love for us,
steady over aeons of time.

In the fickleness of our will, in the doubtings of our minds, in the betrayals
of our hearts, we can scarcely believe in your steady presence through the
years. Startle us afresh. Take our breath away. Renew our trust.

OUR HATRED OF GOODNESS

Refrain: With the wealth of your generous love,
melt the ice of our hating hearts,
dissolve our envy and bitterness,
assure us that we are beyond price.

The spirit of hatred eats us alive,
gnawing away, draining our energy.
With what twisted and mocking delight
the innocent are corrupted, the gentle are scarred.

We accumulate the goods of this world,
"our wealth a reward for our virtue."
Yet we look down from a superior height,
despising the poor, increasing their burdens.

Never content with the possessions we have,
greedy for more, we harden our hearts.
Restless envy peers out from our eyes,
so cold, suspicious, and harsh.

Some of us turn our hatred within,
believing we have no worth of our own.
Cool disapproval drove us to despair,
and we kill ourselves by degrees.

Goodness incarnate was too much to bear,
showing us how crabbed and bitter we are.
The rage to kill rose in our throats,
a satisfaction hollow and bleak.

You took to yourself, Compassionate God,
all our hatred and spite.
You endured with a passion unbroken,
you left us with nothing but love.

Refrain: With the wealth of your generous love,
             melt the ice of our hating hearts,
             dissolve our envy and bitterness,
             assure us that we are beyond price.

So you impel us to justice,
generous in giving, caring for others,
no longer grudging and grim,
able to share with no need to control.

Help us, just and generous God, not to project perfection on to those who
lead us, nor give others the illusion that we ourselves are perfect. May we
leave no room for envy and hatred, and no longer howl with glee when the
good let us down.

THE ENERGY OF COMPASSION

Refrain: Alleluia! We dare to give praise to God.

As the light of dawn struggles through the gloom,
as the sun filters through the morning haze,
as the weary stretch into another day,

As the noonday sun burns and does not relent,
as the pressure mounts on the brain,
as the elderly nod through the afternoon,

As the shadows lengthen and the day declines,
as the air cools around the homeless,
as a night of grieving looms,

As we grow angry at senseless violence,
as we cradle the wounded in our arms,
as we patiently repair the damage,

As the sloucher straightens his back,
as the poor rise up from the scrapheap,
as the barren at last conceive,

As Sarah, Rebekah, and Rachel give birth,
as Ruth follows Naomi to a new home,
as Rahab and Tamar find their place in the story,

As we seek to deepen our trust,
as we glimpse the power of compassion,
as we see the divine in the outcast,

As we remember the tales of our ancestors,
as we recall the moments of freedom,
as we renew our strength at its source,

Refrain: Alleluia! We dare to give praise to God.

As the Spirit of awe overtakes us,
as the depths of compassion overwhelm us,
as the glory and splendour overshadow us,

As we worship at all times, in all places,
as we lovingly relish the Name,
as the people sing with one voice.

*As we seek to discern how to bless you, O God of Power and Compassion,
in all the circumstances and through all the events of our lives, keep our anger
within bounds so that it does not destroy, and keep our caring truthful so that
we do not allow ourselves to be destroyed.*

THE GOD OF EXODUS

Refrain: Alleluia! We give praise to the God of rescue.

We are slaves of a pitiless ruler,
bowed down by an alien language.
We cry to you, O God, in our distress,
and you rescue us by your servant Moses.

We ourselves become your sanctuary,
the people with whom you dwell.
You call us to live in your image,
even as the One who shows us your face.

Even Nature responds with awe
at your power in acts of redemption.
The sea and the river retreat in panic,
the whole creation assists our rescue.

The mountains quake and the rocks splinter,
the sheep and lambs quiver with fear.
Amazement grips us as the scene unfolds,
this theatre which resounds with your presence.

Dance, O earth, at the appearance of God,
turning your anguish to a paean of praise.
Your rocks are turned into pools of water,
solid flint into a flowing fountain.

Nothing is fixed, nothing secure,
when you lead us into freedom.
The gods of nature crumble,
the noise of the powers is stilled.

O God, your greatness is awesome,
your incomprehensible grace in our rescue.
Our voices combine with those of the earth,
we give you the glory for ever.

Refrain: We give praise to the God of rescue.

For now the very earth herself is our home,
a secret not known to the powerful.
For our God was born in a cave,
and was killed cast out of the city.

You owned not a single possession,
and yet the whole world is yours.
Only the one who can never be exiled
is free at the last and always at home.

With exuberant delight and a touch of fear we remember the stories of our ancestors, and we rejoice in you, O God, for you are still the God behind all the powers, with infinite compassion and grace rescuing us from all that enslaves us. Call us out of our imprisonments. Rescue us. Lead us to freedom.

IDOLS AND THE LIVING GOD

Refrain: Alleluia! We praise the Beloved, God beyond gods.

It is not to our name that praise is due,
but to yours, eternal God of Love,
for you are faithful and kind and merciful,
surpassing us all in wisdom and care.

Our idols are silver and gold,
the gods of money rule in our land.
They have mouths and utter platitudes.
They have eyes and see not the poor.
They have ears but hear no cries of pain,
they have noses and keep themselves clean.
Their hands touch no one with love,
their feet never walk the streets.
Keep us from growing to be like them,
may we put no trust in possessions.

Renew our trust in you, O God:
give us courage to face our enemies.
You remember us and you bless us,
you bless all who hold you in honour.

Creator of the universe, God beyond gods,
you give us the earth to care for.
You are far beyond our imagining,
yet you bless each one of your little ones.

Those who are dead to your love do not praise you,
nor those who are gripped by one of the powers.
Keep our love and our freedom alive,
that we may praise you with joy and delight.

Free us, redeeming God, from all that would hold us fast, from all the addictions to which we could fall prey. Keep us compassionate and firm with others and ourselves, that together we may inhabit a land of true liberation.

DEATH LOSES ITS STRANGLEHOLD

Refrain: Alleluia! Praise to the God in whom death is no more.

You have heard, O God, the strains of my distress,
even the silent crying of my heart.
I love you because your ear inclined to me,
I know you were there for me in the day of my trouble.

The cords of death entangled me:
the snares of the grave held me fast.
Tentacles wrapped themselves round me,
crushing me to anguish and pain.

Desperate for air I called out:
Help me. Deliver me. Rescue me.
My strength is sapped, my energy draining away.
With my last breath I cried out in panic.

In your healing compassion you came to me,
with the kiss of life reviving me.
At my very last gasp you held me,
you snatched me from the jaws of the grave.

You delivered me from the stronghold of death,
you wiped the tears from my eyes,
you saved my feet from stumbling,
and I walked free in the land of the living.

How can I ever repay you, O God,
for all the gifts of your gracious love?
I will lift high the cup of salvation,
and give thanks for your holy name.

From time to time you rescue me, O God,
by the skills of your people, by means unknown.
You come to me in the guise of strangers,
I am humbled by their willingness to care.

But what of the people who perish?
What of the children who are wasting away?
Can you save us through the days of our dying,
through the river of no return?

Yet you are the God not of death but of life,
no power can withstand the power of your love,
All that frightens us shrivels in your path,
the trail that was blazed by the Pioneer.

Living Christ, decisive clue to the Love that has no end, renew in us the
steady hope that even the power of death cannot keep us from your presence.

A QUIET MOMENT OF PRAISE

Refrain: Alleluia! We whisper our praise.

A fragment of prayer from the psalmist of old,
Let all the people praise the name of our God.
So now in a quiet moment of praise
our gratitude whispers on the gentlest of breaths.

Not always with jubilant shouts
do we sound our thanksgiving and joy.
From the depths of a silent heart
comes a word but softly spoken.

Secure in the lovingkindness of God,
knowing the Love that always endures,
transforming the evils we face into good,
we waft the breeze and adore.

*O God of Silent Loving, keep us from the trap of believing that the louder
we shout the more genuine is our faith and the more fulsome is our praise.
Keep us aware that love is fragile and vulnerable and that we know it best
in the silence of the heart.*

THE MERCIES OF GOD ENDURE

Refrain: Alleluia! We give thanks for the mercies of God.

Let us give thanks for the goodness of God,
let the people of old shout their joy.
Let the children yet unborn hear its sound,
the harmony of a people of praise.

In the dangers we face you are with us,
you came as one of us and set us free.
We need you no longer on our side,
for your love has spread over our enemies.

Yes, I long for the downfall of those who oppress me:
with the ache of sorrow I remember their harm.
But my bitterness has warmed to compassion,
my anger channelled for justice.

I take my refuge in your presence, O God,
putting no trust in rebellious powers.
The mighty of the earth are not worthy:
humble them to a place of repentance and trust.

When all the powers surrounded me,
in your name I drove them back.
When they swarmed around me like bees,
in your name I drove them back.

I was pressed so hard that I almost fell,
but your power surged through my arms.
For you are my strength and my song,
and have become my salvation and rescue.

So we bound up the rebellious powers,
and gave them into your care.
Take from them their desire for revenge,
and heal their deepest hurts.

Refrain: Alleluia! We give thanks for the mercies of God.

No one shall die and be forgotten,
not one of the little ones is lost.
If the hairs of our heads are numbered,
who can doubt the compassion of God?

We shall not die but we shall live,
and rejoice in the deeds of our God.
Even though you test us to the limit,
you do not abandon us to death.

Open for us the gates of the city,
the city of harmony and peace.
Together restored we enter them,
singing our songs of thanksgiving.

The stone which the builder rejected
has become the head of the corner.
The very ones we despised
are known as your specially beloved.

This is the festival day,
the day you have made for our joy.
We shall be glad and rejoice,
feasting with laughter and song.

Blessed are those who journey in your name:
the light of our God has guided them.
They join the throng in the places of praise:
indeed you are God: we adore you.

*May we not be stingy in our gratitude nor grudging in our praise. Loosen
our stiff bodies to be exuberant and joyful. Let us dance with delight and see
the sparkle in the eyes of God.*

WALKING IN GOD'S PATH

[*God's invitation to us is to follow Christ. It is a journey into Love, along a path that is rarely smooth. The Way is rough, the Truth is costly, the Life is sacrificial. The gate through which we are drawn by Love is always narrow.*]

The journey	The stony road
The invitation	Follow the Way, the Truth, the Life
The implication	Enter by the narrow gate

Blessed are those who are honest in their ways,
who walk in the paths of God's Law.

Blessed are those who treasure God's Wisdom,
who seek God with all their heart.

Those who do no evil deeds
are those who tread the way of Justice.

Dear God, you have given command
that we diligently hold to your Word.

May my ways be kept steadfast
on the narrow road of your Love.

So I shall not be confounded
while I respect the whole of your Counsel.

I shall thank you with unfeigned heart
as I learn to be guided by your Spirit.

I shall hold fast to your Truths:
do not utterly abandon me.

DELIGHTING IN GOD'S WISDOM

[*The path is tough, and, despite boundary marks, we wander from it. We become self-centred; we ignore others on the path. We are constantly invited to love others as Christ has loved us: that degree of love is not easy for it challenges us to bless, pray for, and help those who are hostile to us.*]

The journey	Boundary marks
The invitation	Love one another as I have loved you
The implication	Do good to those who hate you
	Bless those who curse you
	Pray for those who abuse you

How shall the young find their way?
By guarding the boundary of your Word.

With my whole heart I have looked for you:
let me not wander from your Commandment.

Your Truth have I hidden within my heart,
so that I should not fail to love you.

You are blessed indeed, dear God:
teach me your Wisdom.

With my lips I have been telling
of all the Judgments of your mouth.

I have had greater delight in the ways of your Loving
than in all manner of riches.

I will dare to contemplate your Countenance,
and I will deeply respect your Ways.

My delight will be in your Counsel,
and I shall not forget your Word.

LONGING FOR GOD'S JUSTICE

[*As travellers into God we need guideposts which can be discerned from within the words of the Gospels. For example, we are blessed when we hunger and thirst for the right relationships longed for by a just God. Only by being faithful to such wisdom will our lives be built on rock.*]

The journey	Guideposts
The invitation	Be faithful to what I have said
The implication	Build on rock

Deal bountifully with your servant,
that I may live, and keep your Word.

Open my eyes that I may see
the wondrous things of your Law.

I am a traveller upon earth:
hide not your Guideposts from me.

I am consumed with a very fervent desire,
a longing that I have for your Justice.

You have rebuked the pride that lurks in me,
you rescue me when I am lost and astray.

Take away from me the spirit of scorn,
hold me fast to the rock of your Truth.

Keep me from suspicion and hatred:
rather may I meditate on your Counsel.

For your Sayings are my delight,
and they are my counsellors.

ENDURING IN GOD'S WAY

[*When the way is dusty and hot, it is easy to feel weighed down and oppressed. We have then to stop and dig deep in the desert until we discover springs of refreshing water. We also need to learn to receive nourishment from other travellers, as much as in our turn give to them.*]

The journey	Water
The invitation	Let living water flow in you
The implication	Feed the hungry
	Give water to the thirsty

My soul is weighed down like lead:
revive me according to your Word.

When I told you of my ways, you heard me.
Teach me your Wisdom.

Help me to understand the Way of your Love,
and to meditate on the wonders of your Deeds.

My soul droops for very heaviness:
refresh me according to your Promise.

Take from me the way of lying,
and graciously teach me your Truth.

I have chosen the way of faithfulness,
and your Justice is before my eyes.

I cleave to your Law:
let me not be put to shame.

I shall run the way of your Commandment
when you have set my heart at liberty.

DESIRING LIFE IN GOD'S SPIRIT

[*We are called simply to follow, but with deep desire and not with reluctance. It is not a path of human cleverness, but of the Spirit of Wisdom. So we are to turn our eyes from envy of others' success, and turn them towards those who are needy.*]

> *The journey*   Following
>
> *The invitation*   Receive the Holy Spirit
>
> *The implication* Give to everyone who asks you

Teach me, dear God, the Way of your Truth,
and I shall follow it to the end.

Give me understanding, and I shall keep your Law,
I shall keep it with my whole heart.

Lead me in the path of Wisdom;
to do your Will is my deepest desire.

Incline my heart to your Love,
and not to envious greed.

Turn away my eyes from vanity,
and give me life in your Spirit.

Establish me in your Promise,
be faithful to those who are in awe of you.

Take away from me the rejection that I fear,
for your Justice is good.

See, my delight is in your Commandment:
quicken me in the power of your Word.

KEEPING GOD'S WORD

[*To keep on being steadily steadfast in God's Truth even when afraid of the*
powerful—this is to walk in a sacred manner. It is possible only if we
dwell in God's Love. We shall be so delighted in God that we shall not even
want to condemn those who would harm us.]

The journey	Walking
The invitation	Abide in my love
The implication	Judge not and you will not be judged
	Condemn not and you will not be condemned
	Forgive and you will be forgiven

Let your steadfast Love spread over me, dear God,
even your salvation, according to your Promise.

So shall I have an answer for those who taunt me,
for my trust is in your Word.

Take not the Word of your Truth utterly out of my mouth,
for my hope is in your Justice.

So shall I always keep your Law,
for ever and ever the ways of your Love.

And I shall walk at liberty,
glad to fulfil your Commands.

I shall speak of your Wisdom and not be ashamed,
even among the powerful of the earth.

My delight shall be in your Counsel,
which I cherish with joy.

I shall lift up my hands in your Presence,
and listen deep within for your Word.

REMEMBERING GOD'S PROMISE

[*We go astray from the path. We pursue wordly wealth at others' expense, we despise the weak, we even betray friends. To remember God's Promise to be with us always, to ask that we may embody the Spirit of Christ, to contemplate and treasure Wisdom: only so do we renew our pilgrimage.*]

The journey   Astray

The invitation   Ask in my name

The implication   Do not lay up for yourselves treasure on earth

Remember your Promise to your servant,
in which you have caused me to put my trust.

It is my comfort in time of trouble,
for your Word has given me life.

In pride we despise one another:
may we not shrink from your Law.

Let us remember your Justice, O God,
and we shall be strengthened.

May my anger be cleansed by your Truth,
as I confront betrayal and wrong.

Your Sayings have been my songs
in the house of my pilgrimage.

I have thought upon your Name in the watches of the night,
and I have treasured your Wisdom.

It has been for my blessing,
when I have lived by your Commandment of Love.

ENJOYING GOD'S PRESENCE

[*We are enlivened and encouraged on the journey by companions – literally those with whom we eat bread. Even the stranger is to be welcomed as one who also belongs to God. We are to taste and see the goodness of the One who gives us living bread.*]

The journey	Companions
The invitation	Eat of the Living Bread
The implication	Welcome the stranger

Dear God, you are my portion for ever:
I have promised to live by your Spirit.

With heart and longing I come into your Presence:
show me your steadfast Love, according to your Word.

I call your Truth to remembrance,
and turn my feet to your Way.

I make haste, and prolong not the time,
that I might keep your Commandments.

The cords of the ungodly ensnare me:
may I not forget your Law.

At midnight I will rise to give you thanks,
because the Judge of all the world acts well.

I am the companion of all who are in awe of you,
who are guided by your Counsel.

The earth, O God, is full of your steadfast Love:
O teach me your Wisdom.

RECEIVING GOD'S GRACE

[*Fortified by God and by one another we journey on. Knowing that we are accepted as we are, we can the more readily accept and forgive others. We have received the gracious and truthful presence of God, far more enriching than all the world's wealth.*]

The journey	On course again
The invitation	Forgive the sins of others
The implication	Forgive to seventy times seven

Dear God, you have given me grace,
and so fulfilled your Promise.

Teach me true understanding and knowledge,
for I have trusted your Word.

Before I was afflicted I went astray,
but now I keep your Counsel.

You are good and gracious:
O teach me your Wisdom.

Through pride I tell lies against my neighbour:
keep me to your Truth with my whole heart.

My heart grows fat and gross:
let my delight be in your Love.

It is good for me that I have been afflicted,
that I may learn your Wisdom.

The Sayings of your mouth are dearer to me
than thousands of gold and silver pieces.

LETTING BE IN GOD'S HANDS

[*We are misled if we think our hard travelling earns us anything as of right.
We have to take time to stand still and do nothing, to let go of our concerns,
and to let be in God's hands, simply to trust and be thankful.*]

The journey	Standing still
The invitation	To do the work of God is to believe
	in the One whom God has sent
The implication	Hold on to your life and you will lose it
	Let go of your life and you will find it

Your hands have made me and fashioned me:
give me understanding that I may know your Mind.

Those who fear you will be glad when they see me,
because I have put my trust in your Word.

I know that your Judgments are right,
that in your faithfulness you have caused me to be troubled.

Let your merciful kindness be my comfort,
according to your Promise to your servant.

Let your loving mercies come to me, that I may live,
for your Love is my delight.

Let my pride be confounded, with its twists of deceit,
and I will meditate on your Wisdom.

Let those who fear you turn to me,
that they may know your Truth.

Let my heart be found in your Counsel,
that I may not be ashamed.

CLINGING TO GOD'S FAITHFULNESS

[*The vision with which we started out seems to shrivel. Eyesight and insight grow dim. We harm rather than help one another. At best we doggedly endure, clinging to the faithfulness of God who encourages us with Christ's victory over all that would drag us down. Feeling stripped to the bone, we are yet called to clothe one another.*]

The journey   Stumbling

The invitation   Be of good courage: I have overcome the world

The implication Clothe the naked

I faint with longing for your salvation:
with hope I still cleave to your Word.

My eyes grow dim with watching for your Promise,
saying, When will you comfort me?

For I am like a wineskin shrivelled in the smoke,
yet I do not forget your Wisdom.

How long must your servant endure?
When will you judge those who oppress me?

Yet I too have laid traps for others,
and I have not obeyed your Law.

All your Commandments are true:
they challenge our falsehoods and deceit.

We have almost made an end of ourselves upon earth:
draw us back who have forsaken your Way.

Quicken me in your loving kindness:
and I shall keep the Counsel of your Spirit.

TRUSTING IN GOD'S PURPOSE

[*In the very midst of constriction the vision is renewed. Sustained by the eternity and reliability and promised fulfilment of the purpose of God's Love, nourished by the blood-red wine of the very life of God, we continue to walk with our burdens, simply following the Way.*]

The journey	Vision
The invitation	Live in the True Vine
The implication	Take up your cross and follow me

Dear God, your eternal Word of Love
endures for ever in the universe.

Your Truth stands fast from one generation to another:
you have laid the foundations of the earth, and it abides.

In fulfilment of your Purpose it continues to this very day,
for all things serve you.

If my delight had not been in your Wisdom,
I should have perished in my trouble.

I shall never forget your Truths,
for with them you have given me life.

I belong to you, save me,
for I have sought your Counsel.

Many are the traps that could destroy me,
but I will meditate on your Law.

I see that all things come to an end,
but your Commandment is exceeding broad.

LOVING GOD'S TRUTH

[*We miss our way if we do not become childlike in our trust and delight in the tastiness of God's gifts. Even the commandment to love in a tough, enduring, non-possessive way is as honey to our deepest selves. We come to relish the Wisdom, Counsel, and Truths of God.*]

The journey	Honey
The invitation	If you love me keep my commandment
The implication	Become like children

Dear God, how I love your Wisdom:
all day long is my study in it.

Your Counsel makes me wiser than my adversaries,
for it is always in my heart.

I have more understanding than my teachers,
for I meditate on your Word.

I am wiser than the aged
because I keep your Truths in my heart.

I hold back my feet from evil ways,
that I may obey your will.

When I do not turn aside from your Way,
I know that you are my Guide.

How tasty are your Sayings to my mouth,
sweeter than honey to my tongue.

Through your guidance I learn understanding:
therefore I hate all evil ways.

BEING GUIDED BY GOD'S LIGHT

[*The Way becomes obscure, but there is sufficient light once our eyes are accustomed to the dark. We may not realize that we are being guided in a particular direction, but the shepherd's crook is kindly prompting. We may be troubled, but an imperceptible inclination of the heart in prayer is all that is needed for our calming.*]

The journey	Lantern in the dark
The invitation	Let the Good Shepherd guide
The implication	Pray simply

Your Word is a lantern to my feet,
a light searching out all my ways.

I have sworn, and am steadfastly purposed
to keep the Way of your Justice.

I am troubled beyond measure:
give me life, dear God, according to your Promise.

Accept my offerings of praise,
and teach me your Truths.

My life is always in your hands,
and I do not forget your Law.

The ungodly have laid a snare for me:
may I not swerve from your Commandment.

Your wisdom have I claimed as my heritage for ever,
it is the very joy of my heart.

I incline my heart to your Counsel,
always, even to the end.

BRINGING EVIL TO GOD'S JUDGMENT

[*We try to avoid the refining fire of God's truth. We resist the pruning of our self-centredness. We are unfaithful to our promises, we are cunning in our self-deceits, we become weighed down with our vain pursuit of earthly security. Even while hating hypocrisy, we practise it. Only through the astringent love of God will our greedy and inordinate desires cease, our lust for possessions fade.*]

The journey	Refining fire
The invitation	Be pruned, and be fruitful
The implication	Do not look lustfully

I hate all doublemindedness and hypocrisy,
but your Law do I love.

You are my defence and my shield,
and my trust is in your Word.

Away from me, all desire to do evil:
I will keep the Commandment of my God.

Uphold me according to your Promise, and I shall live:
let me not be disappointed of my hope.

Support me, and I shall be safe:
my delight shall ever be in your Wisdom.

Relentlessly expose my unfaithfulness;
may my cunning be in vain.

Rake out ungodliness from me like dross,
for I desire your refining Truths.

My flesh trembles in awe of you,
and I am afraid of your Judgments.

SERVING GOD'S WILL

[*As servants of the will of God, called to love God's wisdom as a precious jewel, we begin to discover that indeed possessions are of no account. We appreciate the wealth that comes to us through enjoying the smallest and simplest acts of kindness, given and received. No earthly greatness could ever compensate for such true treasure.*]

The journey	Possessions of no account
The invitation	Wash one another's feet
The implication	Whoever would be great among you must be your servant

I have done what is just and right:
do not give me over into the hands of my oppressors.

Make your servant delight in all that is good,
that the proud may do me no wrong.

My eyes waste away with looking for your salvation,
for the fulfilment of your righteous Promise.

Embrace your servant in your steadfast Love,
and teach me your Wisdon.

I am your servant: give me understanding
that I may know your Counsel.

It is high time that you acted, O God,
for your Law is being destroyed.

How I would come to love your Commandments
beyond all gold and precious stones.

Therefore I direct my steps in your Way,
and all false steps I utterly abhor.

REJOICING IN GOD'S LOVE

[*God's Love is reliable, steadfast, constant. In that knowledge we can walk firmly, freed from the weight of oppression, with a light step. Even in frightening places, it is as if we are already in the safety of the sheepfold. Living in the spirit of that freedom, we are more able to draw alongside those who are constricted by illness or imprisonment.*]

The journey   Burdens fall away

The invitation   Come in by the Door of the Sheepfold

The implication   Visit the sick and those in prison

Your steadfast Love is wonderful:
therefore I treasure your Wisdom.

When your Word goes forth
it gives light and understanding to the simple.

I opened my mouth and drew in my breath,
for my delight was in your Counsel.

Look upon me and show me kindness,
as is your joy for those who love your Name.

Keep my steps steady in your Word,
and so shall no wickedness get dominion over me.

Relieve me from the weight of oppression,
and so I shall keep your Commandments.

Show the light of your face upon your servant,
and teach me your Way.

My eyes shed streams of sorrow
because folk heed not your Promise.

THIRSTING FOR GOD'S JUSTICE

[*Freed from the weight of worldly expectation and possessions, humbled and poor, even, like a grain of wheat, dying unnoticed, the followers of the Way are the only ones who can know what it would be like to see God's justice, God's commonwealth, established on earth. They cry with yearning to see right prevail. They strive to make it so.*]

The journey   Humbled and poor

The invitation   Let the grain of wheat fall into the earth and die

The implication   Yearn and strive to see right prevail

You are righteous, O God,
and your Judgments are true.

The Ways that you have commanded
are just and true.

My zeal has consumed me
because my enemies have forgotten your Words.

Your Promise has been well tested,
and your servant loves and delights in it.

I am small, and of no reputation,
yet I do not forget your Wisdom.

Your righteousness is an everlasting righteousness,
and your Law is the Truth.

Trouble and heaviness have taken hold of me,
yet my delight is in your Justice.

The righteousness of your Will is eternal:
give me understanding, and I shall live.

URGENTLY NEEDING GOD'S GUIDANCE

[*Nevertheless, it is not easy to keep our sense of spiritual direction. We are easily misled and we have to face the malice of the frightened. We shall lie awake at night, seeking to settle our hearts and wills on God. We shall urgently pray for guidance in the day. We may be given the gift of God's peace, but we shall do well to strive with our enemies sooner rather than later.*]

The journey   Awake at night

The invitation   Receive my gift of peace

The implication   Make friends quickly with your adversary

I call with my whole heart:
hear me, O God, I will keep your Commandments.

Urgently do I cry to you:
help me, and I shall follow your Way.

Early in the morning do I cry out to you,
for in your Word is my trust.

My eyes are awake in the watches of the night,
that I might meditate on your Promise.

Hear my voice according to your steadfast Love,
quicken me, in fulfilment of your Will.

They draw near who persecute me with malice:
they are far from your Law.

But you, O God, are near at hand:
for all your Counsel is true.

Long since have I known of your Wisdom,
that you have grounded it for ever.

CHERISHING GOD'S COMMAND

[*Not one of us can plead innocence or perfection. There is great contrast between our unfaithfulness and the steadfast love of God. This is painful truth. Only by immersing ourselves in God's Love, only by sharing the cup of affliction which was drained to the full by the only One who was indeed whole, can we be given the life that we desire. On the way we have to deny ourselves much of what we now hold dear.*]

The journey	Aware of painful truth
The invitation	Drink the Cup
The implication	Deny yourself

Look on my affliction and deliver me;
may I not forget your Law.

Plead my cause and redeem me:
give me life according to your Word.

Salvation is far from my wickedness,
when I have no regard for your Commandments.

Great is your loving kindness, dear God:
give me life, for such is your joy and delight.

There are many who trouble me, my adversaries:
may I not swerve from your Way.

It grieves me to see our unfaithfulness
when we ignore all that you promise.

Consider how I cherish your Wisdom:
give me life, according to your steadfast Love.

Your Word is eternally true,
and your Justice stands fast for ever.

STANDING FIRM IN GOD'S COUNSEL

[*If we keep to the Way shown to us, we shall discover the treasures of the Wisdom of God—Love, Truth, Peace, Saving Health, Justice. We are invited to trust and not be faithless, to open all the devices of our locked hearts to God. Then we shall be at peace, be able to absorb and reconcile conflicts, and be makers of peace.*]

The journey	Treasure discovered
The invitation	Be not faithless but believing
The implication	Be a maker of peace

The powerful oppress me without cause,
but my heart stands firm in awe of your Word.

I rejoice in your Love
more than one who finds great spoils.

As for lies, I hate and abhor them,
but your Law do I love.

Seven times a day do I praise you
because of the Justice of your Way.

Great is the peace of those who treasure your Wisdom:
nothing can make them stumble.

I have looked for your saving health,
and followed your Counsel.

My whole being holds fast to your Justice,
which I love and long for exceedingly.

Guide me in the path of your Truth,
all the ways of my heart are open before you.

PRAISING GOD'S SALVATION

[*The journey is through a labyrinth. We find our way to our true home by the thinnest of threads. Like bewildered sheep we lose our way in cul-de-sacs of the maze. If we have been found there by the 'angels' of God, then we in turn can at times be a 'presence' of God to others who are confused. In dark and hidden places we can still give, and pray, and fast. And in the end we shall be brought home rejoicing in the God who saves, in and through and beyond our hopes and fears.*]

The journey	Home through the labyrinth
The invitation	Feed my sheep
The implication	Give secretly
	Pray secretly
	Fast secretly

Let my cry come to your ears, dear God:
give me understanding, according to your Word.

See the labyrinth of my ways:
deliver me, according to your Promise.

My lips shall tell of your praise,
for you show me the path of Wisdom.

My tongue shall sing of your Love
and praise your Justice to the skies.

Let your hand guide me,
steady me with the Counsel of your Spirit.

I have longed for your saving health, O God,
and in your Truth is my delight.

Let me live, that I may praise you:
let your Love and your Justice help me.

I have gone astray like a sheep that is lost:
seek your servant, and bring me home rejoicing.

HELP AND HARM

Will I ever be free?

Refrain: Trapped and besieged,
unable to move,
I cry from my prison,
Let my journey begin.

From the days before I knew there were days,
in the darkness of continuing night,
I was caught in an alien country,
my enemy the source of my life.

Bewildered by the smiles of welcome and peace,
nourished, it seemed, for my good,
I lay close to pretence and deceit,
seen only in the light of another's esteem.

I breathed the air of whispered betrayal,
entangled as I was in the voice of the lie.
Infected by words that were bitter and sharp,
it was hard to resist the desire for revenge.

Like a fledgling my whole being trembled,
shaken by my first faltering steps.
At last I could leave the place of my peril,
glimpsing your love which is true and assured.

So you gave me the beginnings of freedom, O God:
the arrows will turn back on those who pursue me,
the burning of the broom tree will shrivel the lie,
my betrayer's heart seared to life by the truth.

Give me courage, Pillar of Flame, as I begin to follow you on the pilgrim
way. Create a calm and glowing centre within me that I may resist the
cruelties of those who seem to love me. May I be firm in refusing all
collusion. May I be harmed no more. Keep my steps steady when I arouse
unresolved conflicts within those with whom I seek to be reconciled. And free
them from their prisons too.

REFRESHMENT AND RIGOUR

Have I the courage to trust?

Refrain: Companion on my journey,
Protector at my side,
I venture on the way
in simple childlike trust.

I look towards the mountain ranges,
and fear their lurking terrors.
The pilgrim path takes me through them,
by rocks and ravines, ambush and vultures.
Stormy winds swirl round the summits,
avalanches threaten across trackless screes.
The hills themselves give no courage or strength,
and I turn once again to my God.

Tempted to slide back into mud,
down to the bliss of oblivion,
yet I hear the lure of my Lover,
whispering through my story's confusion.
The God who draws me is urging me on,
and I discover my faltering Yes.
I stumble along the rough pathways,
surprised by a hand that is grasping my own.

To and fro, back and forth,
on the twists of the journey,
courage moves me onwards,
faith trusts in the future;
wisdom makes me pause,
I rest by the stream;
taking time to delve deep,
I listen for the Voice.

I reach for the unknown mountain,
to the summit where God speaks anew,
on the boundary of earth and heaven,
the frontier of time and eternity,
the place of a special revealing,
marked by the stones of a cairn.
As I ponder the codes of my dreaming,
I am surprised by the mystery of God.

The hills themselves slowly change,
never as firm as they seem;
shrouded, brooding, and dark,
their rocks splintered by frost,
worn away by the lashing of storms,
no strength in themselves to support me,
only from God comes my help.

With the wind of the Spirit empower me,
stirring the substance of earth,
moving my innermost being,
yet keeping me from all lasting harm.
Keep watch, do not slumber, Guardian of your people,
shade from the heat, healer and guide.
Nourish the life of my truest self,
from this moment on and for ever.

*Deepen my trust in your Presence, my God, for you seem often absent and
hidden, and I am afraid of what the way will bring. Deepen my trust.*

PEACE AND PERPLEXITY

What will become of the city?

Refrain: Lift up your eyes and see:
the City of all our dreams.

I was glad when my companions of faith
ventured with me to the house of our God.
Weary and tired, yet our feet will stand
within the gates of the City of Peace,
Jerusalem the goal of our longing,
where the pilgrims gather in unity.

Drawn ever closer to the city,
to the place of prayer and of presence,
to faith renewed and hope restored,
to the healing and peace of the Promise,
we your people climb to the gates,
to the seat of your judgment and mercy.

We pray for the peace of Jerusalem.
May those who love you prosper.
Peace be within your walls,
prosperity in all your households.
For the sake of my kindred and friends,
I will pray from my heart for your peace.
For the sake of the house of our God,
I will do all that I can for your good.

Bless the people of Jerusalem, all who look to Abraham as their ancestor in
faith. Take the energy of our prayers and deeds and transform both place and
people into a city of pilgrimage and peace for the whole world. Bring all of
us there, so that we may taste and see your generous and gracious love.

DELIGHT AND DEVASTATION

Will I survive the piercing eye?

Refrain: We will not be trapped by the eyes of oppression:
we will see with the eyes of our God.

The haughty look of the powerful,
the contemptuous stare of the wealthy,
the cutting glance of the clever,
the mocking glint of the cowardly:

Burdened by eyes that enslave us,
cast down by eyes of derision,
oppressed by eyes that pursue us,
held fast by eyes that never relent:

The eyes of cameras following us,
the shadow of spies in the dark,
the screen displaying the data,
the silent satellite unseen:

Fiery eyes, angry for justice,
compassionate eyes, warming the poor,
courteous eyes, attentive and waiting,
steady eyes, calm and courageous:

A reverent look awed and still,
a ready glance, willing to obey,
a look of hope, expectant of good,
a look of trust, as between friends.

Fill us with the Spirit of Love, All-Seeing and All-Compassionate God,
that we may look with terrible and kindly eyes on those who oppress us, and
shame them to a change of heart and deed.

DELIVERANCE AND DESTRUCTION

Will we weather the storm?

*Refrain: Praise to the God who is for us,
      and for all that is being created.*

If you had not been on our side
when destructive powers rose up and barred our path,
if you had not been committed to our good,
like monsters they would have swallowed us alive.

Their anger was kindled against us,
like the sweep of the forest fire.
Their fury bore down upon us,
like the raging torrent in flood,
the waters of chaos that know no limits,
trespassers that are hard to forgive.

Thanks be to you, our deliverer,
you have not given us as prey to their teeth.
We escaped like a bird from the snare of the fowler:
the frame snapped and we have flown free.

In the joy of deliverance we praise you, O God.
Our hearts expand in a new generosity:
we embody the love with which you create.
Even the powers you do not destroy:
you redeem all our failures to live,
you are strong to bring good out of evil.

*In the dangers and risks of the pilgrim way you are with us, our Companion
God. Strengthen us to face the perils of the powers of storm and hunter that
would overwhelm us, and show us again that your creative love is stronger
than anything else in the universe.*

TRUSTWORTHINESS AND TREACHERY

Are we dependable?

Refrain: We trust the Love that never fails,
the God who stands secure.

Those who put their trust in you, O God,
shall be as if they were Mount Zion itself,
rooted in the depths of the earth,
never to be shaken, enduring for ever.

The mountains stand protecting Jerusalem,
city of ramparts and walls that are solid.
So stands our God around the people,
moment by moment, now and for ever.

So may we be constant and true,
giving no sway to the sceptre of wickedness,
establishing the rule of justice in the land,
lest even the righteous be tempted to evil.

Yet our hidden deceits sap the foundations,
masked by the buildings of goodness and courage.
We are wheat and tares indeed for the sifting,
at the place of judgment and mercy.

O God of Truth, give us the spirit of resistance to the subtleties of evil,
insinuating themselves as we grow stronger on the journey. May we be
honest pilgrims, steadfast, trustworthy, and true of heart, rooted only in
your Love.

EXILE AND EXULTATION

Will we come home?

Refrain: Home at last, contented and grateful.

When God takes us home from our exile,
we shall wake from this nightmare and live again.

Bars of iron will be shattered: we shall walk free
from gulag and ghetto, from dungeon and laager.

We shall sing and laugh for joy,
echoed by birdsong and breeze of the spring.

The land itself will rejoice in God,
the whole world give praise for the wonders we have seen.

Lead us home, renew our hope, bring us to life,
like impossible rivers in the cursed and barren desert.

We go on our way sadly, with tears sowing seeds that will die,
we shall return with joy, with gladness bearing our sheaves.

Restore the years, O God, that we have lost, that the locusts have eaten. Give to us the future that we thought we should never see. Make of the present moment a firstfruit of true liberation. Even when we feel exiled, locked in, despairing, move secretly within us and among us, and without our realising it, keep us moving on our journey to your city.

CARE AND CONSUMPTION

How well are we building?

Refrain: Frustrate our schemes and designs,
yet bless us in city and home.

Eternal God, our Rock and our Foundation,
without you all that we build is but rubble.
Blindly and cheaply we construct on sand,
and the buildings subside and crumble.

Those who guard the city do so in vain;
the watchman cannot see the corruption within.
The lights in the towers shine on through the night,
all for vain profit, soon turning to dust.

Foolish we are to rise up so early,
drawn to the work that consumes us.
The bread of anxiety sours and gnaws at us,
we forget you give gifts while we sleep.

Let us turn to our children and play with them,
'   a glorious waste of mechanical time!
They are our heritage, a gift only from you:
content are those who build steady around them.

Of such buildings is the lasting city made:
blessed are those who delight in such priceless gifts.
They will stand assured when facing their adversaries,
they and their children will grow in stature and wisdom.

Keep us building slowly, steadily, truly. Keep us from being Babel-like,
top-heavy and empty. Keep us building one another up in wisdom and love.
And let us take no anxious thought for tomorrow.

EMBRACE AND EXCLUSION

Do I belong?

Refrain: From our ancestors to our children's children
let us be grateful for the blessings of home.

We are blessed if we hold God in awe,
if we walk in the paths of our Creator.
The labour of our hands will bear fruit:
all shall be well, we shall rest content.

Husband and wife will be happy together,
partners and friends will sustain one another:
in intimacy and trust they will embrace,
and gather to tell tales by the fire.

Children will be a blessing round the table,
guests will bring grace to festival times.
As branches of vine and of olive,
each will be God's presence to the other.

We are blessed if we keep the counsels of God,
who dwells in the secret places of our hearts,
who comes to life between us in love,
who shares bread and wine round our hearth.

God will bless us indeed:
we shall have known Jerusalem –
an outpost of the city of peace,
a sign of shalom on the earth.

Let even the outcast and exile, within us or beyond our gate, not begrudge
the contentment of simple blessings. Let the fortunate open wide their gates
to welcome the outcast and the exile home. In quiet ways may sorrows be
eased and envy dispelled.

GOLGOTHA AND GENOCIDE

Can faith survive?

Refrain: The litany of lament grows loud and long:
The pulse of faith grows weak.

Does the power of the wicked have no limit?
Why do you not restrain them, O God?
Your people of old knew a measure of affliction,
but they praised you for deeds of deliverance.

Their enemies scored their backs with ploughshares,
opening long furrows of crimson.
But you would not let the adversary prevail,
you cut your people free from the chafing bonds.

Their anger welled up within them,
cursing the enemy with withering scorn:
"May they be as grass that shrivels in the heat,
may they never come to the ripeness of harvest."

An easy exchange it seems to us now,
faced as we are with cruelty unleashed –
exquisite refinements of torture's black arts,
children knifed and dumped in the gutters.

Woe to us when to cleanse means to slaughter,
when genocide seems the simple solution,
when bullets explode into a thousand splinters,
when young and old are abused and discarded.

Why do you not act, mute God, in your justice?
How dare we name you as good any more?
We have entered deep darkness in the midst of the journey,
and the pilgrims are paralyzed, unable to move.

We receive no answer to our prayers, Silent God, and yet still we pray to you
lest we despair. Justify your ways to us, and do not silence us, like Job, with
power and grandeur. Convince us again of·the invincible strength of
vulnerable and crucified love, even when Golgotha and genocide seem worlds
apart. Do not fail us in our extremity.

WATCHING AND WAITING

Dare I enter the dark?

Refrain: Costing not less than everything,
        all manner of things shall be well.

Empty, exhausted, and ravaged,
in the depths of despair I writhe.
Anguished and afflicted, terribly alone,
I trudge a bleak wasteland, devoid of all love.

In the echoing abyss I call out:
No God of Compassion hears my voice.
Yet still I pray, Open your heart,
for my tears well up within me.

If you keep account of all that drags me down,
there is no way I can ever stand firm.
Paralyzed and powerless, I topple over,
bound by the evil I hate.

But with you is forgivness and grace,
there is nothing I can give – it seems like a death.
The power of your love is so awesome:
I am terrified by your freeing embrace.

Drawn from the murky deeps by a fish hook,
I shout to the air that will kill me:
Must I leave behind all that I cherish
before I can truly breathe free?

Suspended between one world and the next,
I waited for you, my God.
Apprehension and hope struggled within me,
I waited, I longed for your word.

As a watchman waits for the morning,
through the darkest and coldest of nights,
more even than the watchman who peers through the gloom,
I hope for the dawn, I yearn for the light.

You will fulfil your promise to bring me alive,
overflowing with generous love.
You will free me from the grip of evil,
O God of mercy and compassion.

Touching and healing the whole of my being,
you are a God whose reach has no limit.
All that has been lost will one day be found:
the communion of the rescued will rejoice in your name.

Through the dark despairing depths and the drought of the desert, through the abyss opened up by our failings and folly, we dare to risk our cry to the living God. For you will not let us escape from our greatest good. In our struggle with you, fierce, fiery Lover, let some new glory be wrought, and new and unexpected life come to birth.

CALM AND CONTENTMENT

I shall praise.

Refrain: In quietness and confidence is our strength,
in utter trust our contentment and joy.

Dear God, my heart is not proud,
nor are my eyes haughty.
I do not busy myself in great matters,
nor in what is beyond me.

I am glad I depend on my neighbour,
I make no great claims of my own;
Sealed off by myself I would never know gifts,
never know the bonding of trust.

I have calmed and quietened my whole being,
I am like a child contented at the mother's breast,
in the stillness I look into the eyes of my lover,
I am absorbed in the task of the moment.

It is like the silence of an evening in spring,
made intense by the bleat of a lamb.
It is like the waves of the sea come to rest,
no more than a whisper in the caress of the shore.

The silence and stillness lift the woodsmoke of prayer,
a song of quiet gratitude wafting it high.
Aware of descendants and ancestors with us,
we join the soft chorus of praise.

May we cherish the silence and not be afraid. May we know it not empty
but full of Presence. May the Love at its heart calm our fears. May we know
the gentle touch of a trusting hand.

BEAUTY AND BLISS

I shall wonder.

Refrain: Our gaze is held by your beauty,
we gasp with wonder and praise.

The splendour of the Ark of the Covenant,
housed in the glory of the Temple,
crowning the City of Peace –
the pilgrims were drawn by the beauty of God.

No wonder that David of old
vowed not to enter his house,
to sleep in the comfort of his bed,
till the ark of the presence found rest.

We are stirred by the festival day,
the ark in triumphal procession,
the people decked out in splendour,
the faithful shouting for joy.

Your covenant with your people is strengthened,
your beauty attracting and leading us on,
to the goodness at the heart of your law,
to the truth brought to life in our deeds.

The beauty of carvings in wood and in stone,
of people transformed in their presence,
the beauty of words and of music,
bring us close to the heart of our God.

Yet more was promised to David that day:
a descendant would inherit the Covenant.
Would we be shown a more lasting beauty,
gloriously embodying the divine and the human?

Refrain: Our gaze is held by your beauty,
we gasp with wonder and praise.

And yet – most wonderful paradox –
the beauty of God touched the outcast:
nothing in the Crucified to delight us,
only to faith's eye is God's glory revealed.

If the ugliest of scars can shine with new light,
if you can fashion new forms from our chaos,
if poets can bring hope from genocide's ashes,
we can rejoice once again in the Beauty of God.

*Keep alive in us, Spirit of God, even in desperate days, a vision of a true
and goodly beauty, shaped from the least likely matter of your creation, that
graced and cheered, we may not perish but be encouraged to glory.*

LOVING AND LOVED

I shall love.

Refrain: May we be one in the exchanges of love,
in the look of the eyes between lover and loved.

At oases on the pilgrim way we rest together,
sharing the stories and meals that refresh us.
We remember we are called to be holy, not good,
to do what God requires, to delight in God's blessing.

Brothers and sisters, friends of God,
how joyful and pleasant a thing it is –
like the gathering of a mountain range –
when we dwell together in unity.

It is like a precious and fragrant oil,
like the dew of early morning,
or the scent of summer in the forest –
gifts beyond all expectation.

It is like the very beauty of holiness itself,
a sense of Presence in the places of prayer,
the Godward eyes of faithful people,
the times we are surprised by new blessings.

So we give you heartfelt thanks, O God,
that we can glimpse the harmony of humanity,
that we can trust that all creation will be restored,
that all things will be suffused with the light of your glory.

May we hear your gracious invitation, O Triune God, to share the hospi-
tality of your table and the Dance of your Love, and so respond to all that
you have created for us to enjoy.

BLESSING AND BEGINNING

I shall be blessed.

Refrain: Lead us on, Pillar of Flame,
always moving ahead of us.

We your friends and servants bless you, O God,
as we stand by night in your Presence.
We lift up our hands to the holiest of places,
whose walls pray the prayers of the pilgrims.

To the City of Peace we have come at the last,
and give you, our God, our heartfelt praise.
Bless us and all you have given us,
Creator of heaven and of earth.

Bless us as we turn away from the shrines,
lest by lingering we become pillars of salt,
Even the stones will decay into dust:
the Presence will depart from among them.

Absorbing the gifts our ancestors left to us,
we set out once more on our journey.
What we thought was our goal was but a stage on the way,
and the Spirit is urging us on.

Drawn as we may be by Bardsey and Lindisfarne, by Iona and Durham,
by Canterbury and Jerusalem, by Santiago and Rome, let us take courage
from our ancestors of faith, but let us now seek to make holy the places where
we live and to be made holy ourselves by the God who goes on before us.

SMALL AND GREAT, EXILE AND SETTLER, POOR AND WEALTHY

Refrain: Praise to the God who creates us and calls us,
who promises an abundance of blessing.

We praise you, Beloved, we give thanks to your name;
in the loyalty of friendship we give you praise.
In the house where we heard your promises
we give thanks for the blessings of your covenant.
We praise you for you are gracious and courteous,
we sing praise to your name for it is good.
You have chosen us for particular service,
a priestly people whose love is not narrow.

And you are indeed the glorious Creator,
awesome in your freedom and power.
Your will stretches round the great globe,
echoing to the depths of the seas.
You shine through the fierce heat of the sun,
tempered by the tenderness of clouds and rain.
You howl through the winds of the desert,
whilst giving oases of sheltering green.

You yearn for each of us to have a home,
a piece of the earth to cherish and care for.
Your heart goes out to the wandering exile,
in Egypt, in Babylon, in migrants today.
You lived among us a vulnerable child,
fleeing from the wiles of the powers that be.
You know what it means to be cast out of the walls,
yet you prepare a city beyond our imagining.

Fortunate they are who have houses to dwell in,
whose roots reach far in the ground of the past.
Blessed are those with a language of their own,
through which they can hear your marvellous works.

Refrain: Praise to the God who creates us and calls us,
who promises an abundance of blessing.

Inheritors as we are of an ancient story,
we find our place in the greater world.
Through art and music we are consoled and inspired,
through the touch of our neighbour we know we belong.

Let us not fall into the grip of idols,
dazzled by displays of silver and gold.
Let not our wealth feed a monstrous addiction,
growing tall and slowly destroying us.
Let us live from the point of our need,
of the poor, the outcast, the friendless,
the hurt child who lives in us all,
the needy who bring us the gift of your presence.

Let all the first peoples bless you, O God,
aboriginal, in touch with earth's wisdom.
Let the migrant workers bless you, O God,
nomadic in spirit, with no earthly resting place.
Let the settlers on the land bless you, O God,
who husband the earth for its harvest.
Let the powerful bless you, O God,
who hold the earth in their hands.

Creator of the universe, yet friend to each one of us, giving us our homes, yet
planting in us a yearning for a true and lasting city, disturber of the settled
and comforter of the restless wanderer, may we all come together in your
praise.

LOVE WITHOUT END

Refrain: Alleluia! We sing of your love, now and for ever.

We give you thanks, O God, for your goodness,
for your mercies endure for ever.
By solemn promise you are bound to us,
source of grace for ever and ever.

You are the God beyond gods,
a mystery too profound for our thoughts.
In the shadows of the light we discern you,
we are struck by your dazzling darkness.

You reveal the marvels of the universe
to those who listen and patiently look –
from atoms and genes hidden from our eyes
to the shafts of light from long dead stars.

For the beauty of forms ever-changing,
for the slow turning of the sun and the seasons,
for the miracle of the newly born child,
for the rising of our daily bread.

At the turning points of our lives you are with us,
through times of bewildering change.
At the crossing of the boundaries of the known
by strangers and dreams you encourage us.

You rescue us from slavery and exile,
you are with us on our desert journey,
you give us a place we can cherish,
where the vulnerable find their protection.

You have given us our parts in the story,
from our ancestors whose names are forgotten
to our descendants whose names are not known,
to each a new name in your presence.

Refrain: Alleluia! We sing of your love, now and for ever.

You gave of yourself in the one called Jeshua,
showing us the way of dying to live;
you renewed the gifts of your Spirit,
your glory has shone through your saints.

In you we are bound to one another,
linked by threads seen and unseen,
destined for love in eternity,
when all that has decayed is restored.

In contemplation, discernment, and endurance may we take into the presence of God all that is intractable and unresolved in the life of this planet and its peoples — and in our own lives also — until the time comes when the Spirit of gratitude will spread over all things and for all that has been we shall indeed give our thanks, and to all that shall be we shall sing our Yes.

BY THE WATERS OF BABYLON

*Refrain: Blessed are those who hunger and strive
for all that is just and good.*

By the waters of Babylon we sat down and wept
when we remembered the smouldering city.
We hid our harps in the thickets of the willow;
silently and bitterly we grieved.

They who drove us captive from our homeland
demanded of us a song of our joy.
Goaded by their torment we cried out,
"Sing the Lord's praise in a strange land?
How can we throw our pearls before swine?
You trample on our name, you rob us of hope,
we cannot betray what is holy and precious.
To proclaim what is intimate is to lose it for ever."

It is hard to be faithful and firm,
as despair overwhelms us in torrents.
Troubled we are and uncertain,
no longer assured of God's presence.
O God, do you hear the cries of our hearts
now that we are so far from your city?
On foreign soil can we worship you still?
Have you withdrawn from us for ever?

Yet if I forget you, Jerusalem,
may the hand that plucks the harp wither.
May my tongue cleave to the roof of my mouth
if I do not give Jerusalem my heart's desire.

Refrain: Blessed are those who hunger and strive
for all that is just and good

Great anger rises within me, a thirst for revenge
against those who have destroyed the city.
Even our kin wanted Jerusalem ruined,
stripped bare to its very foundations.
Colonial power and neighbouring tribe
laid us waste with their scorn and their greed.
"May your cities be burnt to a cinder,
your children dashed to pieces on the rocks."

O God, hear the honesty in my rage,
the sharp pain in my heart.
To you alone can I trust the hatred I feel,
knowing you will use it for good.
But how? What to do with my anger?
For its power I need: it must not be taken from me.
"We who have lost so much, hear us.
We who have been so much abused, hear us.
We who now live on the margins, hear us.
We who are denied our own language, hear us."

Yet truly their life has no meaning,
their hearts as hollow as their mockery.
They destroy themselves by their cruelty,
they become as the dust of the city they destroyed.
No, do not let them vanish for ever,
but shame them to repentance and justice.

Work in us all the deeds of your grace.
May we restrain our furious desires,
refusing to be dragged down to their mire.
But keep us from too easy a kindness.
With patient tenacity may we endure,
and keep our anger alive.

Create a new heart in all who oppress,
break down the structures that bind them.
So you will give us the sign that we need
for the grace at the last to forgive.
For now let us mightily strive with our enemies,
until all of us, limping, are blessed.
Together may we sing a new song
as we build a more glorious city.

As cracks split the walls of the houses of prayer,
as the faiths are compromised by collusion with oppression,
as we betray you by killing one another in your name,
as the Spirit of the ages moves on,
challenge us again, Mysterious God,
in homeland or in exile,
in delving within, expecting to be changed,
in anger and truth changing the world,
that we may see beyond the convictions
with which we bind and cage both you and one another,
and having seen, may act.
As no stone was left standing on another in Jerusalem,
so it will be in Canterbury and Rome.
They will fall because their vision is too narrow.
May we not rebuild them as of old,
but keep them as empty silent spaces
that they may speak to us eloquently of what is beyond us.
Empower us to build the City of Peace wherever we are.
May we discern your call to protect and shape
city and home, farm and wilderness, body and community,
all in harmony with your will.
May they alone become temples of your presence,
the places of our prayer,
and the new Jerusalem for which we dream and long.

GOD'S GENTLE TOUCH

Refrain: To those we barely notice
God draws especially close.

Homeless and restless, I sleep on the streets,
huddled in the doorway of the jeweller's store.
Why are they afraid of me who can do them no harm?
Why do they all pass hurriedly by?

A woman stops, eyes steady and clear:
her hand clasps mine, enclosing a coin.
She speaks a few words, spends a few seconds,
risking the laughter of those who pass by.

A man draws close with hesitant step,
embarrassed and awkward when faced with the strange.
Yet he stays long enough to give me some broth,
a waste in the thoughts of those who pass by.

The crypt of a church lies dusty, unused,
till a few catch a vision of a haven of care.
There are some who give food with a listening ear,
a hope unknown to those who pass by.

A few with pure hearts among those who are wealthy
keep stirring the conscience of people with power,
pressing for the changes that justice requires,
sword in the path of those who pass by.

Do they give me a glimpse of an unusual God?
Is there glory in the costly giving of self?
Am I the one God especially loves?
Is God far from those who pass by?

The skilled and the powerful think they are favoured,
they call on their God to buttress their pride.
They miss the gentleness of a touch that is loving,
fearful hands push away and of course they pass by.

We give you thanks, surprising God, with all our hearts. Through the Poor Man of Nazareth who embodied your love, and whose Spirit inspires us still, you keep alive the hope that the true strength of the gentle and merciful will overcome the brittle force of the fearful and powerful, that at the last the unrecognized will indeed inherit the earth.

LIGHT OF LIGHT

Refrain: Always aware of us,
ever-present with us,
ceaselessly creating us —
we respond in love,
we tremble and adore,
our God, mysterious and faithful.

Light of light, you have searched me out and known me.
You know where I am and where I go,
you see my thoughts from afar.
You discern my paths and my resting places,
you are acquainted with all my ways.
Yes, and not a word comes from my lips
but you, O God, have heard it already.
You are in front of me and you are behind me,
you have laid your hand on my shoulder.
Such knowledge is too wonderful for me,
so great that I cannot fathom it.

Where shall I go from your Spirit,
where shall I flee from your Presence?
If I climb to the heavens you are there:
if I descend to the depths of the earth, you are there also.
If I spread my wings towards the morning,
and fly to the uttermost shores of the sea,
even there your hand will lead me,
and your right hand will hold me.
If I should cry to the darkness to cover me,
and the night to enclose me,
the darkness is no darkness to you,
and the night is as clear as the day.

For you have created every part of my being,
cell and tissue, blood and bone.
You have woven me in the womb of my mother;
I will praise you, so wonderfully am I made.
Awesome are your deeds and marvellous are your works.
You know me to the very core of my being;
nothing in me was hidden from your eyes
when I was formed in silence and secrecy,
in intricate splendour in the depths of the earth.
Even as they were forming you saw my limbs,
each part of my body shaped by your finger.

How deep are your thoughts to me, O God,
how great is the sum of them.
Were I to count them they are more in number
than the grains of sand upon the sea-shore –
and still I would know nothing about you –
yet still would you hold me in the palm of your hand.

*Yet my trust falters. I see all that is wrong in the world and in my heart, all
the mutual loathing and hatreds, all the betrayals and lies. Scour our hearts,
refine our thoughts, strengthen our wills, guide us in your Way.*

AGAINST EVILDOERS

Those who defraud the poor of their pensions,
those who deprive the poor of their land,
those who grow wealthy on the backs of the poor:

God of justice and power,
restrain them, confine them, bring them to their knees.

Those who have no coins for the meter,
those who walk far for their fuel,
those whose backs are bent low,

God of compassion and power,
rescue them, liberate them, lift up their hearts.

Those who fly flags of convenience,
those who pollute the rivers and streams,
those who release acid to clouds,

God of justice and power,
restrain them, confine them, bring them to their knees.

Those who sweat in the engine rooms,
those whose health is damaged by their work,
dwellers in forests where the leaves shrivel,

God of compassion and power,
rescue them, liberate them, lift up their hearts.

Those who trade in drugs that destroy,
those who smuggle arms that recoil on their makers,
governments who cynically collude,

God of justice and power,
restrain them, confine them, bring them to their knees.

Those with poison in their veins,
those who will never walk again,
people deprived of their rights,

God of compassion and power,
rescue them, liberate them, lift up their hearts.

Those who with malice slander their neighbours,
those who twist words for the sake of a scandal,
those who use words to boost their esteem,

God of justice and power,
restrain them, confine them, bring them to their knees.

Those who are deprived of their name,
those without value or worth,
those who know not their own language,

God of compassion and power,
rescue them, liberate them, lift up their hearts.

Those who beat the young to submission,
those who torture and rape,
those who violate their children,

God of justice and power,
restrain them, confine them, bring them to their knees.

Children who cower in fear,
all who are wounded and scarred,
survivors who twist in the darkness,

God of compassion and power,
rescue them, liberate them, lift up their hearts.

With the psalmist our anger rises at the harm we human beings cause one
another. We cry out for the oppressed and defenceless — Let the arrogant and
mighty crumble under the weight of their own evil! Let them be plunged into
the quaking mire! Let burning coals rain down on their heads! Let them be
hunted to an exhausted and terror-struck end! Bring them to their knees at
the last, restrained, confined, powerless to harm, at the mercy of those they
have wronged.

IMPOSSIBLE DREAM?

*Refrain: Stretched between anguish and joy,
we live the paradox of faith.*

My whole being reaches towards you, my God:
my heart yearns for your welcoming love.
I would run to embrace you as to a friend,
my voice leaping and singing for joy.

Like incense my prayer rises to meet you,
carried on the breath from my lungs.
My arms stretch out, lifting me high,
seeking the hand that is eager to touch.

To the unheard music my feet start dancing;
embodied in movement I become as my joy.
From the depths of my belly arises a cry,
a glorious Yes to the whole of my life.

O that it were so! It is only a dream,
far from the walls of this imprisoning cell.
Exhausted and limp, I stagger and fall,
my prayer no more than a flickering thought.

Silenced by the greedy and scared,
I have no one to utter a passionate cry,
the heartfelt anguish of the unjustly imprisoned,
from the narrow cells underground.

I scratch my name on the prison wall,
frightened I am losing all sense of my being.
Will no one speak on behalf of the mute,
will not the Judge of the earth do right?

Is the hope of my heart an impossible dream?
Will I ever dance in the rays of the sun?
Will I know the warmth of a welcoming hand?
Will a voice of love ever call me by name?

May the fitful tremblings of our prayer move through the world with compassion to give to someone in prison, neglected and forgotten, at least a moment's respite from despair.

TRUST THOUGH REJECTED

Refrain: Alone and rejected dare I trust,
hearing only the Silence of God?

I call to you, my God, with heartfelt cry:
insistent in my need, I seek your Presence.
Barely do I believe and yet still do I pray,
and make no secret of all my troubles.

When my voice croaks and is faint,
when weariness overtakes me on the way,
do you hear my whisper and know where I walk?
Do you know there is much that makes me stumble?

I am left in the silence with no one to help me,
not even a hand draws close to touch me.
I can no longer speak, I drift in a vacuum,
thick glass hems me in: no one can see me.

With a cry without words or sounds,
I search for your Presence, O God.
Do you still have the power to rescue me?
Do you care enough for my plight?

Save me from all that oppresses me,
from the powers that are too strong for me.
Lift me from the dungeon that confines me,
that I may laugh and sing again.

With generous heart beyond measure,
will you come to my healing and rescue?
Then I shall rejoice in the voices of praise,
and give you the glory for ever.

Rejected and isolated, we seek warmth and affirmation, nourishment and
good company. Come with the wind and the bread, the water and the word,
the fire and the balm.

AFRAID OF DEATH

Refrain: Dissolving into the void,
disintegrating to dust,
I cry out in desperate need,
Deliver me from the fear of death.

My heart is open, I come without guile,
I dare to pray to a God who is faithful.
I cannot justify myself in your Presence;
with trembling I bring my desperate need.
I make no plea for justice,
I depend on your mercy and grace.

The devourer is crushing my bones,
the ravenous hounds knock me to the ground.
the unconscious dark overshadows me;
dumped in the ditch I am given up for dead.
My will to live grows faint within me,
my heart is appalled and terrified.
No longer does the stream flow through me:
my taste is of death, acrid and dry.

I cling to the memories of faith,
my heart once lifted in gratitude.
When I least expected your presence,
with the deepest joy you surprised me.
Let me be calm and reflect on your goodness,
on the innumerable gifts you have given me.

Refrain: Dissolving into the void,
disintegrating to dust,
I cry out in desperate need,
Deliver me from the fear of death.

Trembling I stretch out my hands,
hungry for the food that sustains.
Without you I cannot but perish,
starved in the depths of my being.
Long have I believed you are with me,
however unaware I become.
Do not sever the threads that connect us,
lest I drift into space for ever.

Let me hear of your compassion and mercy,
rising with the warmth of the sun.
Show me the way I should travel,
your kindly Spirit giving me courage.
Deliver me from the shades of death;
for the sake of your name calm me.

Release the grip of the power of death,
disarm all those who oppress me.
May death and death-dealers have no meaning,
shrivelled to dust and transfigured to joy.

Like the disciples of old, we are afraid of the power of the storm that destroys
and terrified of the power of the love that transfigures. May we hear again
the accents of encouragement: Do not be afraid, be of good courage, I am
with you.

THE CREATOR LOVER

Refrain: *O Lover, Divine and Human,*
intimate, insistent, and tender,
courteous in paying attention,
passionate in wholehearted embrace,
bring us alive and alight,
each a singular creation.

Blessed be you, O God our Creator:
you are the source of our power and skill,
you teach our hands to shape chaos,
our fingers to mould intractable clay.
You swive with us in a dance of delight,
creating what is new with your partners.

We seem to ourselves to be but a breath,
our days a shadow that soon passes by,
insignificant in the vastness of space.
But O the wonder and marvel of your touch –
awesome that you should draw so near,
embracing, empowering the children of earth.

You bring us alive with electrifying power,
you touch us with the fork of lightning.
Flesh and blood can hardly contain you,
yet your power does not destroy us.
At the heart of the flame is a tender calm,
in courtesy you never intrude.
Little by little you warm us to life,
and we take part in the work of creation.

Refrain: O Lover, Divine and Human,
intimate, insistent, and tender,
courteous in paying attention,
passionate in wholehearted embrace,
bring us alive and alight,
each a singular creation.

You strive with evil, with destructive powers,
not with the matching of strength,
but absorbing their harm in your dying,
in the expending of love and of life.
Hold us steady when we are faced with chaos and fear,
when the waters foam and rage through the night,
that we may pierce to the eye of the storm,
and know the love that sustains.

So we shall sing a new song,
on flute and trumpet singing your praise.
We and our children shall be people of beauty,
burgeoning with life, maturing to vintage.
The earth will produce in abundance,
the sheep will lamb in their thousands,
there will be no distress of miscarriage,
no loud lamentation in our streets.

*Creator Spirit, surge through us with the thunder of the pounding waves,
breathe through us with the whisper of the evening breeze, dance through us
with the leaping flames of the sun, ripple through us with the merriment of
the mountain stream.*

REGULAR BLESSINGS

Refrain: The rhythm of the drums,
          the beat of the heart,
          reliable and steady,
          the voice of your faithfulness.

For the dawning of the light,
for the sun at mid-day,
for the shade of the evening,
we give thanks to our God.

For the rising of the moon,
for the guiding stars,
for the comets on cue,
we give thanks to our God.

For the breaking of the fast,
for noontide's refreshment,
for the meal round the table,
we give thanks to our God.

For the greening of the woodland,
for the grains of the harvest,
for the fruits in their season,
we give thanks to our God.

For the cry of the baby,
for the flowering of youth,
for the strength of maturity,
we give thanks to our God.

For laws that protect us,
for those on alert,
for the routines of safety,
we give thanks to our God.

Refrain: *The rhythm of the drums,*
          the beat of the heart,
          reliable and steady,
          the voice of your faithfulness.

For the fall of the autumn,
for the quiet of winter,
for the boundary of death,
we give thanks to our God.

For the trust of friends,
for the blessings of home,
for the covenants of love,
we give thanks to our God.

For the unfailingly generous,
for the wisdom of years,
for constant compassion,
we give thanks to our God.

For the hidden who serve us,
for the water and power,
for work taken for granted,
we give thanks to our God.

God of good gifts, surprise us again with how reliable you are. Thank you for the trustworthiness of so many people in their repeated tasks for the benefit of the whole community. We touch a mystery unsearchable and wonderful, the marvel of the everyday. And you, O God, are constant and faithful, abundant in steadfast love, passionate and limitless in the giving of yourself to us and all the world, partners as we are in your covenant of creation.

SOCIETY RESTORED

Justice and Jerusalem

Refrain: Praise to the God of Justice and Peace:
from the depth of our being we praise you.

We praise you, God beyond gods;
with a world restored we praise you.
In faith we anticipate that day,
and praise you for the firstfruits of its coming.

We do not put our trust in passing fashions,
nor in the promises of powerful people.
They are powerless to save, their ashes are scattered,
their words soon crumbling to dust.

To the Creator of the infinite heavens,
of the earth and the seas and their creatures,
who works unceasingly for justice,
we give our heartfelt praise.

You keep faith with your promises for ever,
you put right the wrongs of the oppressed.
You give food to the hungry and thirsty,
you set the captives free.

You give sight to the blind,
your arms lift up those who are bowed down,
you love those who live simply,
you care for the stranger, the widowed, the orphan.

At times we do these things with you,
surprising ourselves by our courage,
giving voice to those who are not heard,
troubling and pressing the makers of policy.

Refrain: Praise to the God of Justice and Peace:
from the depths of our being we praise you.

The cities we know are a patchwork,
a jostling of places of hope and despair.
Yet still we give thanks for the vision
of the City of Harmony and Peace.

In the justice of relationships made right,
in the peace that is well-being for all,
we worship the God of justice and peace,
we praise the God of freedom and joy,
we adore the God of love and new life,
we bless the God of reconciliation and healing,
we glorify the God of harmony and bliss.
We add our voice to the music of God;
we fall silent in the presence of Mystery,
in wonder and awe and love,
the Mystery that is the Source of our being
and the Goal of our longing,
beautiful, utterly holy, glorious light,
unbounded love: Alleluia! Alleluia!

PROMISES FULFILLED

City and Countryside

Refrain: Praise God whose Promise is fulfilled:
it gives us great joy to give thanks.

The earth itself is transformed,
the City of Peace is established:
creatures in their thousands leap for joy,
and the people dance in the streets.

The scattered outcasts greet one another,
kings and clowns tumble together,
the hobbling teach the dancers new steps,
the scars of the wounded shine.

The torn hills heal over with grass,
the gnarled trees put forth new shoots.
Ramblers and farmers take care of the land,
the scattered homesteads dwell in safety.

Protesters and politicians sit down together,
the clever sit at the feet of the wise.
The frantic are calmed by those in wheelchairs,
the sexually diverse are welcomed in love.

The cattle are released from their pens,
the hens run free from their sheds.
The walls of the camps are demolished,
numbers are forgotten and names are restored.

No longer do we glory in the might of our arms,
taking pride in the weapons we polish.
No more is the tallest and biggest the best;
no one even thinks of trampling the weak.

Refrain: Praise God whose Promise is fulfilled:
        it gives us great joy to give thanks.

Women and men bring their gifts to each other;
no longer are they driven to harm and abuse.
In eyes that speak truth they see each other,
and know how to touch in the sparkling of love.

Marvellous rarities are tasted by all,
bread that is wholesome is baked once again.
The water we drink springs clear from the hills,
the finest wines grace every table.

The skaters spiral on the frozen lakes,
the skiers exult on the mountain slopes,
the gliders swoop and soar through the skies,
the surfers ride the thunder of the waves.

Through the artists a world of bliss is unveiled,
through the poets fresh images of truth are revealed,
through the scientist what is hidden comes to the light,
through the lovers unfolds the joy of new life.

Restored, fulfilled, gathered together,
we know we belong to the universe.
In songs of harmony we embrace one another,
transfigured in the Presence of the One who is All.

> *In the celebration that embraces the exile and outcast,*
> *in the joy that sings of freedom at last,*
> *we worship the God of justice and peace,*
> *we praise the God of freedom and joy,*
> *we adore the God of love and new life,*
> *we bless the God of reconciliation and healing,*
> *we glorify the God of harmony and bliss.*
> *We add our voice to the music of God;*
> *we fall silent in the presence of Mystery,*
> *in wonder and awe and love,*
> *the Mystery that is the Source of our being*
> *and the Goal of our belonging,*
> *beautiful, utterly holy, glorious light,*
> *unbounded love. Alleluia! Alleluia!*

CREATION RENEWED

Touched and Transfigured

Refrain: Praise to the transfiguring God,
whose touch transforms and renews.

Let the Alleluias ring out in the dark,
the darkness that dazzles with unfathomable light.
Let the People of the Way sing their praise,
alive in the Communion and Mystery of Love.

The Lover, the Beloved, the Spirit Between,
the Love that cannot but be outpoured,
pulsing, cherishing, urging new life,
astonishing, wonderful, marvellous to see.

The threads binding together this extraordinary love
are gossamer and golden, invisible and strong,
reaching out to connect all creation for ever,
from amoeba to human, from atom to brain.

So diverse and complex is this web that we share,
so many forms to name and delight in,
we needs must choose to focus our praise,
our voices finding words for those who are silent.

Let the sun and the moon and the stars
and the earth and the ocean give praise.
We are bound with them; they belong with us:
all change – must it be to decay?

The mountains levelled to plains are changed;
the oceans bed buckles to rise from the sea;
the rivers carry silt and make the vales fertile,
the snows melt to release the spring.

Refrain: Praise to the transfiguring God,
         whose touch transforms and renews.

Seeds yield their life in the darkness of earth,
the flowers, the fruits, and the grains all grow;
some change in the earth to be seen only at harvest,
their abundance deepening our sense of well-being.

The worms and the parasites, hidden from view,
all work their mysterious ways,
puzzling destruction a prelude to life,
a transformation that stuns us to silence.

All is changed and may seem to be lost,
and we too know death and decline.
Yet working within us, unnoticed, unseen,
is the thread that binds and transforms.

And we touch one another to pain and to pleasure,
our skin so vulnerable, so finely tuned.
Can we reach out and create life with our God?
Can we lose yet discover ourselves?

What once was a curse can become a wise wound,
the hand that abused can caress and be kind,
violation can change to the sharing of passion,
we can be warmed to life by an intimate fire.

Praise, praise above all,
all that is No is transformed into Yes,
Yes to the God in whom we belong,
belong together in the dance of delight.

In the love that has taken and shaped every power,
in the new creation that rises from the totally dead,
we worship the God of justice and peace,
we praise the God of freedom and joy,
we adore the God of love and new life,
we bless the God of reconciliation and healing,
we glorify the God of harmony and bliss.
We add our voice to the music of God;
we fall silent in the presence of Mystery,
in wonder and awe and love,
the Mystery that is the Source of our being
and the Goal of our longing,
beautiful, utterly holy, glorious light,
unbounded love. Alleluia! Alleluia!

RECONCILIATION EMBRACED

Held and Healed

Refrain: Praise to the God who overcomes all divisions,
who bears the pain of our healing.

Blessed are those who refuse to take vengeance,
blessed are those who cause no harm,
blessed are those who break the cycles of slaughter,
blessed are those who bless and do not curse.

Blessed are those who resist the temptations of power,
who refuse to gather it to themselves.
Blessed are the little ones who find new courage
to claim and inhabit their own.

Blessed are those who seek to reconcile,
who themselves form a bridge for strange meetings.
Blessed are those who repent of their oppression,
blessed are the harmed who show them mercy.

Blessed are those who absorb others' hurts,
who refuse to give back in like manner.
Blessed are those who keep in touch with their enemies,
who refuse to let them go.

Blessed are the judges who wisely discern,
who help to put right what is wrong,
who bring together those who are estranged,
at no little cost to themselves.

Blessed are those who use the sword as a scalpel,
to be accurate and clear in their telling of truth,
who protect and probe but do not destroy,
whose wounds serve only to purify and prune.

Blessed is the One who bears the world's pain,
who loves and endures to the end,
who holds to the heart a wincing world,
who surprises us with healing and hope.

In the reconciliation that is based on repentance and mercy,
in the healing that has held and enfolded the pain,
we worship the God of justice and peace,
we praise the God of freedom and joy,
we adore the God of love and new life,
we bless the God of reconciliation and healing,
we glorify the God of harmony and bliss.
We add our voice to the music of God;
we fall silent in the presence of Mystery,
in wonder and awe and love,
the Mystery that is the Source of our being
and the Goal of our longing,
beautiful, utterly holy, glorious light,
unbounded love. Alleluia! Alleluia!

HARMONY CELEBRATED

Sounds and Silence

Refrain: Praise to the Creator of harmony,
in the music of silence and sound.

We praise you, O God, holy and beloved!
We praise you for your glory and wisdom!
We praise you for your creative power!
We praise you for your deeds of deliverance!

We praise you in a glorious symphony!
We praise you on the flute and harp!
We praise you with the caress of the trumpet!
We praise you with the solace of the cello!

We praise you on the quickening horn!
We praise you on the strumming guitar!
We praise you with the pipes of the clans!
We praise you on the deep resounding drums!

We praise you in the unnoticed pauses
that make music of disordered sounds!
We praise you in the depths of the silence,
in the music of the dance between eyes that love!

We praise you for all your gifts!
We praise you for your mysterious being!
We praise you for weaving us together!
We praise you that we belong to the universe!

Let everything that breathes under the sun,
let the voices of our ancestors of old,
let worlds unknown, within and beyond,
all on this glad day give you praise!

In the music that is wrought from the silence,
in the silence where we hear the quietest of echoes,
we worship the God of justice and peace,
we praise the God of freedom and joy,
we adore the God of love and new life,
we bless the God of reconciliation and healing,
we glorify the God of harmony and bliss.
We add our voice to the music of God;
we fall silent in the presence of Mystery,
in wonder and awe and love,
the Mystery that is the Source of our being
and the Goal of our longing,
beautiful, utterly holy, glorious light,
unbounded love. Alleluia! Alleluia!